THE OZ EFFECT

THE OZ EFFECT

The Daniel Gifting for Living Counter Culture

JUSTIN LITTLEJOHN

To My Parents James and Julia Littlejohn,
Who raised me in the ways of the Lord.

ACKNOWLEDGMENTS

First and foremost, praises and thanks to the God, the Almighty, for His showers of grace. Without him life would be vain and empty. I would like to also thank my wife Jamie for being my editor and sounding board, and for putting up with me hopping out of bed and hobbling down the stairs at 3 and 5 AM while working on this book. To my girls and my son Zephaniah; you all are my fuel and my reason to never quit. Thank you for being patient with me as I navigate the new path to which God has led us. I am extremely grateful to my parents for their love, prayers, caring and sacrifices for educating and preparing me for my future. Thank you putting the right things inside of me and preparing me for greatness. You may not have been able to give me everything everyone else had growing up; but you gave me something most people didn't have. It is that very thing that has led me to where I am do today. For that I am forever grateful.

To Barry and the Johnston family. I love you all more than words can say. Since the earliest years of my childhood you have done nothing but add value to my life. I don't think it is possible for me to love a family more than we love you guys. Thank you for a lifelong friendship, prayers, and for always believing in me. To the Cook and Hogle Families, thank you for loving and supporting my family and for seeing the best in me no matter what. Finally, to you the reader; thank you for spending your hard-earned money to support us in this endeavor. I pray that it adds value to your life and that you are blessed by its contents.

Table of Contents

Introduction 1

Chapter 1 – The Oz Effect 3

Chapter 2 – Optical Illusions vs. Clear Perception 17

Chapter 3 – The Daniel Gifting 27

Chapter 4 – Living Counterculture 37

Chapter 5 – Passing of the Scroll 51

Chapter 6 – Modern Day Babylon 61

Chapter 7 – The War on Truth and Sincerity 71

Chapter 8 – Protecting Your Identity 85

Epilogue 103

Notes 107

About the Author 109

Introduction

Welcome to the land of OZ! A land where what seems to be a golden road will take you away from the mundane realities of your everyday life...Ok. You can wake up now..... No, you are not in another world, realistically speaking. However, for some people reading this book metaphorically you are! It may seem like I am playing with words, but I am not. In fact, throughout this book, you will soon come to understand what I am conveying to you concerning my claims. It is imperative that you pay very close attention in the first chapter for you to fully understand the context which will be conveyed throughout the entirety of this book. You're probably asking yourself right now what is the OZ effect? I've never heard of that before! That's ok because to my knowledge no one else has until now. The OZ effect is an allegoric term that represents some key components from the fictional world of Oz. Oz is a make-believe city of possibilities detailed in the famous fiction novel "The Wizard of OZ".

I coined this phrase in this unique manner in order to articulate what I believe to be an apostolic and prophetic word for young adults and young believers in the world today. There are many people in our world with incredible giftings and anointings on the inside of them that God wants to use to change cultures and regions. However, due to the image-obsessed cultures we live in, we have lost sight of who we truly are, thus resulting in an abundance of ineffective cookie-cutter Christians. I hope and pray this book challenges you to seek, find, and accept your giftings and calling and be your best you! You, just like Daniel have been called to live counter-culture! Don't fall for the image, don't settle for less than what God has for you. Accept your giftings and your differences, because it is in your differences that you will make your greatest difference in this world and fulfill the calling of God on your life!

The Oz Effect

As a young kid, I was always a huge fan of the classics. That is something that still holds true with me today. I can remember watching the movie "The Wizard of Oz" as a child. The story always fascinated me. I honestly can't articulate why. Maybe it was because the movie allowed me the opportunity to imagine a life outside of the word I knew growing up. A life with limitless opportunity and impossibility. As I grew older, I still imagined a lot. I would have visions and dreams of what I wanted to be, and the things I wanted to achieve. However, one thing I noticed is that I never gave much thought of what it took to become what I imagined. How about I say it this way, I imagined what I wanted to be; but I couldn't fathom the art of becoming what I wanted to be.

You see, what I didn't understand at that age was that although it's great to dream and imagine, it's more so important to understand that there is a process between the realm of imagination and the road to what you wish to become. The road or path you take to get there is what I would call understanding the "art of becoming".

Today we live in a world where many people are ruled by the image portrayed by the culture we live in or by what the Bible would call vain imaginations. Vain in this context is defined as useless or meaningless. The images and imaginations are considered vain and useless because many times what we imagine ourselves being or doing, is not always what God has graced us to do therefore our fruitless efforts yield forth meaningless results.

Welcome to OZ

Today many young believers and young adults around the world struggle greatly with their identity. In fact, I would say the majority, though many do not care to admit it; question whether they are on the path that God has intended for their life. This confusion in many cases results in the individual feeling lost and frustrated. Once the individual becomes lost and frustrated, desperation kicks in and they begin to doubt the world as they know it around them. It is at this point that they began to imagine themselves in another world. They begin to look at the lives of other people and see themselves being that individual, having their spouse, living in their home. They become so fixated on the world of others so deeply that eventually, the life of another person becomes their identity; thus, resulting in the individual losing sight of their uniqueness, gifting and who God called them to be.

The fictional novel "The Wizard of OZ", by Frank Baum, (1900) begins with a young girl by the name of Dorothy who lives in a one-bedroom house in Kansas. Dorothy is a child who believes that the world she is accustomed to is not suited for her. She seeks a place somewhere outside of her own world, where she can be someone else. One day a cyclone strikes and carries her and her only friend (her dog Toto) away to a land called Oz. When they come from within their home they walk into a world of unique people, of variant style and stature. Dorothy, now desiring to go home, is given a pair of silver shoes and is advised to go to the Emerald City to see the great "Wizard of Oz". It was only the great and powerful Oz who could help her find her way back to Kansas.

Along the way to the Emerald City, Dorothy comes across three additional companions; a scarecrow, who wishes he had brains, a tin woodman, who wishes to have a heart, and the cowardly lion, who seeks to find courage. On their journey together, they come across many challenges but using the scarecrows good sense, the tin woodman's kindness, and the courage of the cowardly lion they finally reach the Emerald City. Upon reaching the Emerald City, Oz is made aware of their arrival. However, he does not summon them for several days after. When the great and powerful OZ finally allows Dorothy and her companions an audience with him, he seems reluctant to grant their wishes. Amid the excitement and suspense, Dorothy's dog Toto knocks over the screen which was before them and suddenly the truth about OZ is unveiled. It was at that moment that they saw OZ for who he was, a fragile, insecure, powerless, commoner just as they were.

Once his gig was up, Oz attempted to salvage his embarrassment by filling the scarecrows head with bran, pins, needles and calls it a brain. Next, he places a silk and sawdust heart within the tinman. Oz then gives a drink to the cowardly lion, which he calls courage. Finally, to Dorothy he agrees to make a balloon that will help fly her back home, unfortunately, the balloon flies away before she could board. Ultimately Dorothy learns how to use the shoes which were originally given to her, she clicks them together and wishes to be in Kansas again and her wish is granted.

The Allegory between our Culture and Oz

Although this brief synopsis may seem irrelevant at first glance, when you analyze the literary context in this novel, it becomes obvious that there are many metaphoric parallels between the fictional characters in this story, to that of many people in today's world. You see, there are many people around the world who just like Dorothy spend days moping around wishing for something or someone to take them out of a life that they are unsatisfied or bored with. For some of you reading this right now, you may be thinking this sounds a lot like me! Though many would not care to admit it, it does not make it any less true. The truth is in the world we live in, everything is image driven. This is the complete opposite of the kingdom of God which is taste driven.

"Oh taste and see that the Lord is Good: blessed is the man that trusteth in him!" (Psalms 34:8)

Taste is different from sight in that sight does not bring about an experience. For example, I can sit at my house every day and look at pictures of the Niagara Falls and admire its beauty but even after doing that I could not tell anyone I have experienced its beauty. Why? Because experience requires a physical connection. To have experienced the Niagara Falls I would have to have personally visited and felt the misty wind from the mighty falls touch my face; allowing me to not only see but yield some physical manifestation of its greatness. On the other side of the spectrum, you have the world, which is image driven.

"For all that is in the world, the lust of the flesh, the lust of the eyes, and the pride of life." (1 John 2:16).

The world we live in is image driven. As scriptures states, all that is in this world is the lust of the flesh, the lust of the eyes, and the pride of life. All these are controlled by what we see. For example, concerning lust of the flesh; many men and women deal with addictions to porn or sexual immoralities. This begins with what they see and offers them fantasy and pleasure but does not allow the true experience of intimacy with a man or woman who will truly love them in the same manner of Christ. Their encounters through such perverted entities a mere image that can appease only the flesh and not the spirit. Likewise, the lust of the eyes. The lust of the eyes is simply an infatuation with what we see, it could fall into lust, but it can also full under covetousness and self-vanity. Finally, the pride of life. This is probably the one that gets most people and keeps us from as early as adolescents, and follows us through our golden years, and for many until we depart the earth. The pride of life is the projection of the image that our life is perfect. It's the hardening of our heart to the fact that something is missing in our lives, yet we cover it with other things to make our life seem happy and joyful. This is the root of most deception in the world.

The Oz Effect Amongst Believers

As I previously explained, the allegory between the culture of this world and the land of Oz. There is also much truth to this in the realm of the church and the lives of many believers; especially new believers and young adults. The Bible says there is a way that seems right to a man, but therein lieth destruction. (Proverbs 14:12) When a man or woman becomes born again, they are scripturally referenced as a newborn babe. (1 Peter 2:2)

For this reason, it is important that the babes are brought up properly understanding their new life in Christ, what it means to follow Christ, discover their gifts, and discover God's purpose and plan for their life. It is important to know these gifts are already inside of these new believers even at the moment of conception. (Jeremiah 29:11) However, the problem is although now saved and a citizen of a new kingdom (kingdom of God) many churches are not properly discipling these newborns and helping them understand the principles of the kingdom of heaven which will help them successfully navigate the kingdom of earth. So why is this happening you ask?

I feel it is a result of the church failing to truly know those who labor amongst us. (1 Thessalonians 5:12) When we as stronger/experienced believers fail to aid new and young believers in understanding their identities in Christ then we unintentionally leave them subject to seek their identity elsewhere. When they are left to fend for themselves, they are left for the god of this world to devour them through the realm of what they see in the natural; robbing their spiritual purpose and identity in Christ. When the church cannot aid them in finding their identity, the world will give them a false one.

Going back to the story, we see that young Dorothy is like many young believers today. She is dissatisfied with where she is at. She has no friends or anyone who understands her, and she believes she has no identity. As these feelings kick in, she begins to imagine herself somewhere else, in an alternate reality where she can find someplace of purpose. It is at this moment that her imagination became vain. Once she arrives in the imaginary land and embarks on her journey to the Emerald City, she discovers there are others like herself. The Tinman, the Scarecrow and the Cowardly Lion, all represent various other young believers. They are on the same journey, battling the same problem, but seeing something different. This same concept goes for Christians without identity and inner peace. The Tinman sought a heart, the Scarecrow a brain, and the Cowardly Lion sought courage. They all sought something different yet something they believed would allow them some sense of purpose or importance.

Before I go any further, I want to allow you, the reader, a moment to ponder this.... I then want to follow with a question. What is it that you are seeking? What is it that you believe you are missing? Or better yet who told you, you didn't already have it? Who told you, you were naked? (Genesis 3:11) As we read in the synopsis of the story, the four would embark on a journey on the yellow brick road which would bring them great challenges and obstacles to which they would overcome all using the same gifts and talents inside of them that they were seeking from Oz. However, during the journey they never realized it. Why? Maybe because no one told them they saw that virtue inside of them. Maybe no one had told the scarecrow he was capable of great ideas. Or told the Tinman how big his caring heart was, or maybe the Cowardly Lion how brave he was, or even Dorothy, how beautiful her life truly was.

So, in your case, maybe you are on a journey to discover what you believe is missing on the inside of you. Or maybe no one has ever bothered to tell you the greatness they saw on the inside of you! Well, I want to let you know it's already inside of you. From the moment of your conception, God gave you everything you needed to do great and mighty works! (Jeremiah 29:11) However, the fact remains that many times we fail to see our gifts and abilities, we only see what we are not or what we don't have. If we are not told differently, we could spend a lifetime seeking from others what we already have. Such is the case for the four main characters of this story. Later we see after their arrival to Emerald City, at the pivotal moment and conclusion of their dreams coming true; that an unlikely character would reveal the truth behind the curtains of the man they thought could give them what they wanted. That character was Toto, the dog.

I want to pause here and say that it is important for us to remember that many times in life it is what we least expect, which brings about the very thing we seek. For Elijah, it was the raven that brought food to him in a cave, for the blind man it was mud and Jesus's spit on his eyes that brought his sight. Scripture states that it is for our good that God works in such ways. This is how he confounds us or gets our attention when we are caught in our foolish desires. (1 Corinthians 1:27) In the case of this story, the foolish thing was the dog knocking over the screen. However, it was this very action that resulted in the truth revealed; that Oz was a normal commoner, a man with no power. The great and powerful Oz was, in fact, a fraud, a figment of their imagination!

Defining the Oz Effect

So, you may be thinking to yourself right now, ok, I see what you are saying. There are good metaphors and correlations between this story and the world we live in but just what exactly is the "Oz Effect"? Well, allow me to explain. In order to understand what I have termed the "Oz Effect," you first must understand the purpose of OZ. The purpose of Oz is to appease the imaginations of the vain. So, in all reality, an Oz can be whatever you make it! For some, Oz is a person, for others, a career. Ultimately an Oz can be any vain imagination or any high thing that exalts itself against the knowledge of God. (2 Corinthian 10:5) Oz is anything that allows you to believe it has the power to give you something that God cannot give you! That's why it's vain! The fact that Oz's are exalted against the knowledge of God negates the very power they seek to project. When the curtain is pulled back, what looks to be a powerful image ends up being nothing. However, by the time you realized you have been fooled, months and years of your life can be taken. So, then the "Oz Effect" can best be defined as the blinding of our true power and identity by an image or imagination of what we believe can give us what we already have.

Oz in the Flesh

While I believe in talking about the spiritual aspect of the "Oz Effect", it's only fair to also address its tangibility or manifestation in the flesh. All around the world, in every arena there are Oz's walking amongst us. These "Oz's" are people who project power, control, and domination over others they deem inferior or controllable. Furthermore, the individuals mentioned above are typically powerful, talented, or skilled themselves, but have mastered the ability to manipulate the gifted into believing that they are unable to achieve success without them. As a result, many people spend years of their life going to a job building the businesses, empires, and legacies of other many of which are Oz's (not all). What's even crazier is that this also occurs in the church as well.

What allows Oz to manifest so effectively in the world and the church is because just like we see in the story, Oz hides well. The image which Oz projects is so strong and so powerful that it intimidates those seeking an audience with it. Furthermore, Oz is a master of seclusion. They do not lead from the front. Why? Because it would expose the fact that the image of themselves, they are projecting is not real. Instead, they become effective in controlling people behind the scenes and having them do their bidding while they remain secluded, playing God with the lives of others. However, when the curtains fall and they are exposed, they are revealed for what they truly are; powerless and ineffective leaders. Always remember effective leaders are genuine and transparent. They can lead from the front because they have nothing to hide. An Oz will use the image or projection of power to string you along, and when you figure it out, it will cover its embarrassment with consolatory efforts. If you are seeking to be great find a transparent leader to train and teach you, never submit yourself to the influence of an Oz.

Conclusion

The "Oz Effect", quite a unique name. Maybe it will stick, maybe it won't. Nonetheless, don't get lost in translation on the name, because what will stick is the truth! That truth is that many people in the world are walking aimlessly, chasing images and imaginations which culture says they must be or what they believe will fill the voids and empty spaces in their lives. What a sad deception.... What we really must come to understand is that there is a God who formed us and placed incredible gifts and abilities inside of us before we were conceived. Whether or not we discover and walk in those abilities and callings is up to us! Don't bow down to the image of who the world says you must be! You have the option to seek the image of what the culture and your imagination say you need, or to seek the master and creator of the universe to walk in what he has given you. The master workman who formed you and holds the blueprint to your very being has given you all things pertaining to life and Godliness. In the chapters to come, we will examine this topic more from the life of one of the greatest prophets in the Bible. A man who influenced an entire culture through his ability to discern visions, images, and dreams. It is this discernment that will empower us to change culture.

Keys to Remember:

- The "Oz Effect" is the blinding of our true power and identity by an image or imagination of what we believe can give us what we already have.

- The culture of this world is led through sight or image. The culture of the kingdom of God is through taste or "experience" of the Lord's goodness.

- No matter what the Oz's of our culture set before you, there is nothing they can offer you that God has not given you.

CHAPTER 2

Optical Illusions vs. Clear Perception

As a child, I was an avid reader. I enjoyed reading as a way to get outside of my own mind, into the world of another person. I can remember vividly when the school would have the yearly book fair. Even though I couldn't afford to buy any books, just the thought of the 30 minutes in the library scanning through "Hank the Cow Dog" and "The Hardy Boys" books filled my heart with excitement. However, one day I stumbled across, a book unlike any other I had seen before. Keep in mind at the time I was in third grade. The book had such an impact on me that I still remember it to this day. This book was a book full of optical illusions. I can remember turning the pages and being astonished as illusion by illusion played trick after trick with my eyes, causing me to doubt my perspective in what I was truly seeing.

Optical Illusions

An optical illusion is an image that uses color, light, and patterns to create images that can be deceptive or misleading to our eyes; which result in our brains being fooled or mislead. In its simplest form without the illusion aspect there lies the word optical or shall we say optics. Optics can be defined as the science of light. Nearly everything we use and enjoy on a daily basis is brought to us by the science of optics, these things range from the cameras on our phones, blue-ray DVDs, and even television. Furthermore, the physical aspect of optics is found in the way in which it interacts with matter. You see, light has a unique ability to reveal what lies in the deepness of the dark. Thus, allowing us to see things we would normally not be able to see with the naked eye. These things range from technologies that allow us to film and capture images, and even map and explore various galaxies in outer space! Although there is an incredible, natural, God-created aspect of optics, there are also spiritual aspects that must be understood by believers to successfully navigate their way through the dark culture ruled by the God of this world (Satan). It is important to understand that if our natural optics were switched to let's say 100 percent transparency into the spirit world, what we would see would be quite terrifying to most believers.

Paul writes to the church of Ephesus that we wrestle not against flesh and blood but against principalities, against powers, against rulers of the darkness of this world. (Ephesians 6:12) Understand Satan is the God of this world. His kingdom has a structure there are various rulers of dark regions and they operate inside those who yield themselves to the power of his authority. In fact, the people who have seen these demonic beings describe them as hideous disgusting, foul looking beings.

There are many true stories out of Hollywood in which musicians, actors, and entertainment icons, have been interviewed on camera speaking of their interactions with the realm of darkness. I will spare the names but if you search it will not take long for you to find them. I have personally seen interviews of artists speaking of having sex with the devil or mermaids, sacrificial rituals; and unfortunately, even the selling of their souls. Sadly, many of these musicians and stars had their beginning's in the church. But the allure of the world or the lust of the flesh and the eyes caused them to become blind and forsake their calling. I often reflect on how and why these things occur. How does one grow up in church serving God with their ability and then just walk away into a world of darkness?

One extremely successful female music artist described her journey towards darkness. In an interview that I watched, she stated she grew up in a home in which her parents were ministers. She had lived inside the realm of ministry her entire life and even became involved in the Christian music scene. However, due to having very little success on the Christian music charts, she began to move away from her Christian roots and released her first debut album under a secular record label. After the release of her debut album, she became an entertainment staple and climbed the ladder of the entertainment industry. Today she is not only still making chart-topping records, but she has also been a staple on numerous television shows. Examining her life, I can't help but wonder two things, why? and how? In the same interview, she shared her life openly. I can remember her crying and talking about her two identities and how one of her identities dominates the identity of the person she knows she truly is… This is heartbreaking. It truly grieves my spirit to know her personal state but also that she is not alone; as this is the case for many people today.

The Dark Angel

Although at times many Christians mean well, I believe that if we are not careful, we can be a bit too abrasive, especially when it comes to assessing the whys and why not of another's actions. As I stated before, I think often of how many saved talented artists find themselves in a situation in which they commit suicide or live a life in which they can afford everything but personal happiness. When assessing such things, I believe that we as believers must truly understand that this is spiritual. The Bible says the kingdom of heaven suffers violence, (Matthew 11:12) which means that the kingdom of light and the kingdom of darkness are constantly at war. So how is the devil able to come from the realm of his kingdom and extend his influence on the lives of others? Through an image, or we can even say an optical illusion. In (2 Corinthians 11:14) the Apostle Paul writes that Satan himself masquerades as an angel of light! Think about that! Satan is not light, but he has the ability to appear as light, especially to those who don't have discernment. As we learned before it is light that bears the true power to reveal and interact with matter. Satan must masquerade as light in order to interact with us in the natural realm. It is through his masquerade that Satan is able to create lies in our minds which poison our spirits. He cloaks his deception by manipulating those lies into the form of images, pictures, depicting fame riches, happiness, and success. So, for the untrained spiritual eye, these things look great! They look beautiful! Satan is truly a master deceiver, the great optical illusionist.

Clear Perception

In his first letter to the Church, the Apostle John wrote, "This is the message we have heard from him, (Jesus) that God is light and in him, there is no darkness at all". (1 John 1:5) God truly is the light of the world! Because of this, as we learned in discussing optics, God as the creator and light of the world has the ability to reveal anything and to interact with all matter. This can range from calming a raging sea for his fearful disciples, or literally blinding Paul (then Saul) on his road to Damascus to persecute

Christians. Jesus the light of the world is truly the revealer of all things.

Picture Perfect

There are many things from my childhood that if you asked me about, I have buried so far in memory, I wouldn't be able to tell you much about it. However, what I can remember clear as day, is the first time I went to summer camp at Fort Courage in Alabama. Even as I write, I can't help but reminisce on the sights and sounds and all the incredible people I met. There were truly some picture-perfect memories of which I will never forget. As camp ended, I remember all the kids getting together and taking pictures with the friends they had made. In the mid to late 1990s the instant cameras were at the height of their popularity, so all the kids had them. I can remember getting my camera and taking picture after picture while winding the little knob from 25 down to zero. Once I had used up all the photos, I had packed my camera to take it to Walmart to have the film develop.

When I got my photos back, I noticed the envelope was very thin. I was certain that something strange had occurred, so I walked to the customer service desk. I informed the attendant that I had taken 25 photos but somehow, I only ended up with 11. She then asked to see the envelope, so I handed it to her. Suddenly she reached inside the envelope and pulled out a white piece of paper with a note on it from the photo processor and proceeded to read it to me. The note said that the lighting was not right on several of the pictures and on most of them they couldn't be made out at all. As I listened to her words, my heart sunk into my stomach. I had lost over half of the greatest memories of my life at the time.

However, twenty-some-odd years later, from spiritual lenses, I can now see why so many people are having a hard time obtaining clarity for life. It's not the absence of life or living, it's the absence of light. It may sound simple, but the fact remains, it is light that allows us to visually make out in darkness what we could not otherwise do. When our lighting isn't right, we cannot create the perfect clarity in the events which occur in our lives. However, by walking with Jesus we walk in the light as he is in the light, (1 John 1:5-7) this ensures that we are submitted to the lordship of Jesus thus allowing him to lead us to green pastures and deliver us from all evil; even the evil that is attractive to our flesh. It is through the light of our fellowship with Christ that we can maintain an accurate perception in life.

The Trojan Horse of Life

One of the greatest tales and illusions recorded in history occurred during the Trojan War in the city of Troy. Troy was a city known for its impeccable ingenuity and its grand, impenetrable walls. During this time the Trojans had been at war with the Greeks for about 10 years and the war soon became a siege of the great city. Over time attrition began to set in and a Greek King named Odysseus developed an idea to deceive the Trojans that he believed would allow them inside of the great Trojan gates. Odysseus being a military tactician, ordered the Greeks to construct what many historians believe to be a horse like structure made of wood. They would make this structure big enough to place Odysseus and a host of Grecian soldiers inside. The remainder of the Grecian army would create the idea that the Greeks had retreated and left the horse as a homage to the Trojans for a hard-earned victory. When the Trojan royals awoke and saw the monument, they threw a city-wide celebration. The king ordered the structure brought inside the confines of the city walls, to be paraded around before the people. However, as the people were sleep, king Odysseus and the men inside crept from inside the horse and opened the gate of the city. The Greek army then rushed inside, and the great city of Troy was overtaken.

Now I'm not sure if the Greeks decorated this story for increased glory or if it happened exactly as it is taught in historical accounts. Regardless of its origins, there are great spiritual principles that can be drawn from this historical event. You see, in our lives, it is what we desire most in our hearts that can be disguised by Satan as a Trojan Horse and used to destroy us. That's why Jesus must be the desire of our hearts. We must seek his kingdom then all the secondary desires of our hearts will be met. When we attempt to reverse that order, we expose ourselves to optical illusions and Trojan horses. These horses will appear to us in the form of our wildest dreams, they will appear as right. However, the result of them will be destruction. This is the ultimate objective of Satan is to kill steal and destroy you. Satan seeks to abort the call of God on your life using the very things you seek and love. That's why we as Christians must continually walk in the light of the Holy Spirit so that we can avoid the schemes of the enemy and not fulfill the lust of the flesh (Galatians 5:16).

Conclusion

One of the quickest ways to find yourself a victim of the Oz effect is to fall for the optical illusions that Satan places in front of you. As a young adult or even a young believer, there are so many void and unknown paths in which you will be faced with every day. It is important that we remain under the Lordship of Christ as he is a lamp to our feet and a light to our path. (Psalms 119:105) It is only in fellowship with him that we will be able to see beyond the images and illusions. It is the light that reveals the hidden things which will show us our path and God's perfect will for our lives. Thus, wherever we go that light goes, that power will follow allowing us to become agents of change in a culture of darkness. Be light as he is light!

Keys to Remember

- Optical illusions are what you believe you see; accurate perception is given through revelation by Jesus Christ as you walk with him.

- Satan masquerades as an angel of light, however, he is the king of darkness. Satan's "false" light is only a cloak of destruction.

- Never allow Trojan horses inside your walls (spirit). Remember a true blessing of the Lord maketh rich and addeth no sorrow.

CHAPTER 3

The Daniel Gifting

Textual Shifting

Throughout the first two chapters of this book, I aimed to set the stage by solidifying the truth of a very foundational issue of mass deception. This deception plagues not only the culture of the world but also many young believers in the church. It is my prayer that by now that I have clearly articulated this issue in a manner that stirs your spirit to continue reading. From this point on the book will now shift from the metaphoric and allegoric to the apostolic and prophetic realm.

The Daniel Factor

In the field of mathematics, a factor is considered a number that was broken down into individual numbers from a whole number. Those factor numbers can then be multiplied together to equal that number. To explain in a manner easier to understand, some numbers can be broken down into smaller and separate numbers but

27

when multiplied together still become that original number. They are forever systemically linked to that number. A good example of this can be the Holy Trinity. The Father (God) the Son (Jesus) and the Holy Ghost are their separate beings who operate independently yet are unified as one. In the world we live in today we are seeing deception in all shapes and forms on levels that have never been seen before. As I pondered this very thing, I believe it was at that moment that I became convinced without a doubt that the Lord wanted me to write this book. You see, when you become a believer, you immediately are enlisted into the army of the kingdom of God. What's unique about an Army is that they all have a variety of capabilities. The variety exists to allow the military the ability to fight off various attacks such as land, air, sea, space, etc. The sum of all these capabilities would be the military term "combat power".

God, the General of our great army is the supplier of these weapons. Each soldier is equipped with unique giftings and abilities which allow that believer to effectively fight off the attacks of the enemy and claim regions for the kingdom of heaven. No soldier has the same fight, every soldier is not placed on the same battlefield, but we are all fighting the same war. The war against principalities, powers, and the rulers of darkness in this world. One of the most unique soldiers in the Bible was a young man by the name of Daniel, who was placed on the battlefield of enslavement by the Babylonians. As a slave his name was changed to Belshazzar, he had a new language placed upon him, and was taken from the temple where he had once freely worshiped God and was placed into the presence of blasphemers and idolaters. Daniel like Dorothy was thrust into a world and a culture, unlike anything he had ever seen. It is for this reason that God equipped Daniel with tools that would not only sustain him but would also result in his ability to impact his culture in a mighty way.

Babylon the City of Wonder

While deeply pondering the life of Daniel, I found that one of the most interesting aspects of his life was the setting for which his experience began. Unlike most situations when a nation is forced into slavery, Daniel was not beaten, chained, or dominated. Instead, he was set aside for his looks and demeanor and placed into the king's palace as a wise man and a liaison. Furthermore, he was offered a daily portion of the king's meat, and the same wine which the king drank. However, what the king did not understand was that Daniel had purposed in his heart that he would remain separated and consecrated unto God. Now I don't want to go any further without putting this whole Babylon captivity setting into perspective. Babylon was at that time one of the most beautiful places on the earth. In fact, its hanging gardens were considered one of 7 wonders of the ancient world. Babylon was a city full of incredible sights and sounds, very appealing to the lust of the flesh and eyes. This was not a situation in which Daniel was to be a lowly poor servant. He was offered what most people in America could ever dream of; The finest, food, drink, clothes, and prominent position. It is these variables that make Daniels' story so powerful.

Before being allowed to appear in the palace the King instructed the master of his eunuchs (Ashpenaz) to ensure that Daniel and his counterparts, now named (Shadrach, Meshach, and Abed-Nego) to be well fed so that when they appeared before the people they would look well and strong. However, Daniel purposed in his heart that he would not defile himself with the king's meats and luxuries. (Daniel 1:8) When the chief of the eunuchs saw that Daniel would not eat the meat, he pleaded with him to comply. However, Daniel because of his favor was able to work out a deal that would allow him, Shadrach, Meshach, and Abed-Nego to eat vegetables and water. When the ten days, had passed Daniel, and the three who fasted appeared better and healthier than those who had consumed the king's delicacies. Because of the miraculous results of Daniels fast, the chief of the eunuchs took away the delicacies of the King and gave the other non-believing wisemen vegetables and water as well. Wow! How incredible is that? And to think this is only of the beginning!

The Daniel Gifting

At the beginning of this chapter, I discussed factors, and how they are components of whole numbers that when multiplied together once more become that number. Now it's easy to say, well that's numbers. What does that have to do with anything related to human life or better yet the spiritual realm? My answer is everything! You see, we serve an awesome all-knowing God, a God who knows what you will need before you even ask for it (Matthew 6:8). God knew every hardship ahead of Daniel. God knew every threat, challenge, and obstacle he would face. For this reason, God instilled in him several factors that when multiplied together and used as such become his gifting. Consider this passage:

"As for these four men, God gave them knowledge and skill in all literature and wisdom; and Daniel he had understanding in all visions and dreams." (Daniel 1:17)

From reading this passage we see that God gave Daniel:

- Knowledge
- Skill in all literature and wisdom
- Understanding in all visions and dreams

Each of these factors were individually operational but when they were combined created an incredibly powerful synergy which resulted in what I have termed the Daniel Gifting of discernment.

What the Lord has Shown Me

Before writing this book, the Lord began to speak to my spirit concerning the millennial generation. At the time he spoke to me, I was serving as a college and young adult pastor at a church in Huntsville, TX. I was deeply impressed with the level of openness and transparency of the college students. I had been heavily involved for over 6 years with college and young adult ministry at the time, but I had never seen a group of kids so hungry for the truth as I saw in this young group. I can remember vividly how to open these young adults were with me and my wife. They would speak to us about everything from parental and relationship issues, to deep issues with addictions and temptations. Also, I had never been so spiritually utilized in my entire life, weekly we were bombarded with prayer request and inquires as to the interpretation of scripture and an assortment of other various spiritual inquires; it was truly the hungriest group of college students for the things of God I had ever seen.

One of the first things I felt the Lord reveal to me was that the word curses against the next generation needed to end. I began to ponder all the things I had heard about the millennial generation from teachers, on the news channels, and sadly even the church. Although I did not particularly struggle in this area, I still doubled down to ensure that when I spoke concerning the next generation, my words were words of life. Next, the Lord began to show me that many millennials had become disheartened. These reasons ranged from being victims of bad parenting, lack of discipleship and even the mass amount of hypocrisy found amongst many leaders in the church. These and several other factors have begun to play a major role in the turning away of our young people from the things of God. Over the next month or so the Lord began to give me messages regarding seeking and following. He began to reveal to me that this generation was truly crying for revival. They were seeking discipleship, someone who would be there Paul and model before them what it meant to truly follow Christ. This is something I taught very intensely on every Wednesday as in my spirit I could clearly see the many ways the kingdom of darkness was waging war against them. I don't remember ever hearing the Lord so clearly as I did during that "Discipleship Series" I taught. It was at the conclusion of that series that then I received in my spirit one of the strongest and most direct words concerning young adults.

I was meditating one morning, and it hit my spirit that much of the millennial generation is not this rebellious group of wicked degenerates bent on living in sin. Many of them have come from broken homes and families and witnessed failed marriage after a failed marriage and broken promise after broken promise. Also, they have gone to places such as churches seeking wisdom and direction only to find that many of the people leading them are not modeling the character of Christ. It is these unfortunate occurrences that have led to many young adults turning away from the faith. Before I decided to begin this book, the Lord showed me that just like Daniel, many young people have been born into worlds and cultures and circumstances which are not of their own doing. As I previously stated, God in his great wisdom has already given us everything we will ever need in life. We must learn how to be sensitive to his spirit which will increase our ability to operate in these gifts. God knew that as a prophet in a wicked culture, Daniel would need to be a quick study. He also foresaw the dream that Daniel would interpret and the writing on the wall at the dinner before Daniel would even translate it. Because of this foreknowledge, God graced Daniel with unique abilities or factors, that he would later use to spread the knowledge of the power of God to his captors.

Conclusion

Having said that, God is still in the same business today! God sees the threats that lie around and ahead of you, he understands your fears, needs, and desires. He has seen your future. Because of this, God has placed unique abilities inside of you that when added and multiplied with each other combine to become your gifting. In today's world ruled by image and false perception on a level never seen before; God is beginning to unleash a downpour of unique giftings on the next generation.

These giftings will allow young adults to see beyond the images and deceptions of fame, lust, pride, and many other snares. In addition, theses abilities will empower them to win hundreds and thousands to the kingdom of God. As we continue to dive deeper into the life of Daniel; we will see not the complete purpose of these giftings. We will also see a measure of gifting that allowed insight not only into the secret things within the Babylonian culture but also of a world that would exist millenniums after his death!

Keys to Remember:

- God has placed unique abilities and gifts inside of you, the totality of these abilities is your gifting.

- In the last days, the Lord is releasing a Daniel gifting. This gifting consists of several factors but when conjoined together equal the gift of discernment.

- The Daniel gifting is the ability to not only see, interpret, and understand but also allows the power to change culture.

CHAPTER 4

Living Counterculture

"For we are in this world but not of this world. If you were of the world, the world would love its own. Yet because you are not of the world, therefore the world hates you." (John 15:18-19)

This scripture has been used as the focal point of many Sunday morning sermons all over the world. I can remember hearing such messages as a child but not understanding its full context entirely for many years. In my mind, I was in this world. I went to school like other kids, I ate, I played video games; I was just a normal kid looking to find his place in the world. While that may seem simple; the truth is if you asked most new believers, young adults, or youth what it means to be in the world but not of the world; most would say, "to not behave how the world behaves". Although this answer bears some truth; being in the world and not of the world was not merely spoken by Jesus as a form of behavior modification to his disciples. No! It was instead a strong preparatory statement solidifying the fact that the disciples would not just live out their purpose in this world with peace, but

37

they would suffer for being different in a world which would not accept them. From this, it is clear to see that the words of Jesus in (John 15:18) were not directed at behavior but were instead directed at a culture.

Culture is defined by Merriam Webster's Dictionary as the beliefs, customs, arts, practices of a particular society, group place, or time; also: the characteristic features of everyday existence such as a way of life. The English definition alone solidifies the fact that culture, though including behavior; exceeds way beyond it. In fact, to further bring it into its proper scriptural context, let's examine the world further. The Greek word for culture is Politismos. If the stem and the root of the word are separated it would appear as Poli-tismos. Poli, meaning city/assembly; and tismos, meaning civilization. Civilization is probably the most interesting of the two words, as it is defined as the stage of human and cultural development in which an organization that is considered most advanced. The findings of this word study when used accordingly allow us to reveal the proper context to which Christ was speaking when he was addressing his disciples in this famous John 15 passage. Jesus was not telling his disciples that they were aliens or from another world. Jesus was not telling them to live a life of seclusion or separation from society, as that would violate his own commission of world evangelism which he would give them. No! In this passage Jesus is telling them that they are not OF the world, not from; because they were in fact from this world. However, now as disciples of Christ, their kingdom, their culture, their way of life was different. They were now called to a lifestyle of what I call counter-culture!

My First Counter Culture Experience

Some might ask, so what is counter-culture exactly? That is a good question. It also will likely depend on who you ask. For some zealous believers, their view of counter-culture is to buck the system and fight against any and everything the world does. This usually results in a good person, with good intentions being rejected and ineffective in making true lasting change. I can remember as a kid being a huge fan of cartoons with superpowers and mystical characters. Now whether you believe these shows to be harmless or demonic in nature, I leave to your interpretation. However, I can remember when our parents found out a group of us had been playing the games and dealing the cards.

I can't tell you how it all transpired but I can tell you that our parents were not the least bit thrilled. One day after church they went through the house and turned mattresses went through drawing pads and had us throw away any and everything that had to do with any of these shows. I am not saying this in any way to demonize either mine or my friends' parents but instead to shed light on an issue that would set me back for years. You see at the time we were just kids, and, in our minds, we were just doing what kids did. We had no clue we were doing anything wrong and did not have any spiritual understanding or discernment to know if what we were playing with was perceived as evil.

As we grew older and transitioned into our mid-teen years, we began to lose our child-like egocentric personalities and began to grow into independent teenagers. However, with our newfound socio-psychological developments, we would once again witness the same treatment. I can remember being a young man immensely gifted with an abundance of musical talent. I would drum on any and everything I could possibly drum on. Because of my love for drums, I and several of my other friends in the youth group developed a love for heavy Christian rock. We would skateboard around town and listen to music like Skillet, Project 86, Underoath, Emery, and several other hardcore bands. I want to add that the culture of our youth group at the time was either convert to rap and the hip-hop culture or go elsewhere. I can remember us asking a member of the youth leadership team, why do we always have to listen to rap or hip-hop? The response we usually got was that there were evil spirits behind the music that we listened to; and that it sounded "worldly". It confused me and upset me so much because there was just as much of a "worldly" sound in the Christian hip-hop as there was in the heavy Christian rock we were listening to. Our youth group at the time was around 50 teens on a Wednesday night. We were active, went on mission trips in Europe and Mexico and traveled around the area dancing and ministering at churches. It was truly a great experience. However, over the next couple of years, we would see a drastic change.

The shifting first started when a teen of Caucasian descent informed his parents what was going on. His parents then began discussing the issue with other parents who then approached the youth pastors. The situation then began to escalate as more ostracized teens began to speak up. Despite the grumblings from the disgruntled youth, the culture remained relatively unchanged. As a result, teens began to leave the youth group. Some stopped going to church altogether while others began seeking other places to worship. The culture went from a range of ethnical diversity to an all-black culture in a relatively short period of time. A youth group that had so much diversity, gifting and talents went from great to nearly nothing because of an attempt to root out what the leaders at the time believed to be evil.

Having shared such an experience, I want to convey that my reasoning for sharing this experience was not for the purpose of singling out the mistakes of others or to be dishonorable in any way. My intent is to clearly convey the dangers of misconception concerning counter-culture. There are truly good people, with good intentions, who in attempts to create culture, end up self-destructing the very thing they are trying to create due to lack of understanding as to what counter-culture is.

What Counter Culture Isn't

The stories I shared from my childhood experience are very mild examples of an issue that has truly plagued the modern church in the day we live in. Christians, most of whom I will say mean well have made attempts to change the culture of today's world but are failing due to the same issue that resulted in the deterioration of my youth group. What I noticed about churches (and I have been to many around the world) is that many Christians are like immune systems. When they see a germ or sickness, they attack it in hopes of removing it from the body. However, if not careful this can result in the attacking of vital organs which will further threaten the health of the body in its entirety. To further explain let's examine Lupus. Lupus is an autoimmune disease in which the body's immune system mistakenly attacks the organs under the notion that they are a threat to the internal wellbeing of the body. Because of this mistaken disease, many people who suffer from this disease face the possibility of organ failure, transplants and even sadly, the possibility of an untimely death. I have learned through personal experience and through many interactions with Christians that at times if we are not careful, we can become the autoimmune issue of society rather than the cure it needs to bring about the kingdom culture of Christ.

Though most of us may mean well and are full of passion in zeal, I think it's safe to say many of us have missed the mark on what it means to live counter-culture. I can remember when I first got radically on fire for God. I was heavily involved as a student leader in our college ministry. I would passionately walk the Sam Houston State University campus inviting people to church and talking to anyone who would listen about Jesus. However, once I got the students to come to my Bible studies or to the college services, I struggled to relate to them on an intimate level, better yet on any level. It's like they would be drawn to me, and then I would lose them. Over that year, I began to ask myself why I would hit it off so well with many of them, only to lose favor and fellowship with them months later. I soon began to realize that the source of my limited effectiveness as a result of many things I had unintentionally learned as a young kid and as a teenager. You see my experience had taught me that to live radically for God everyone I was discipling had to know what I believed was wrong and what was right. That my opinion mattered. Just as it was with me then, the same issue is present today. Many Christians' influences are overshadowed by their opinions.

To further explain, I can remember hanging out at the pool one night with some students after college service.

These students were not churched much if at all and very few of them would be considered young believers at best. Amid our discussion, somehow, we came to a discussion about politics. That conversation soon branched into controversial issues such as abortion, homosexual marriage and several others of which I cannot recall. I remember boldly stating my political position and opinions as if I was taking a bold stand for Christ against the wicked culture of the world. I thought for sure the students would be touched, blessed and influenced by hearing my strong beliefs and opinions but unfortunately, that was not the truth. The conversation soon grew argumentative and the atmosphere tense. Although I would maintain friendly relationships with these students until they graduated, the dynamics of the relationship were never the same. From this disappointment, I began the practice of self-assessment. I had to ask myself, did they really need to know all that? Did I really have to give them all my life's opinions and beliefs in one setting? What did I even accomplish? Did they feel inspired when they left my presence, or overwhelmed and suspicious of me and my intentions?

From this discipleship failure I learned that if I was going to be effective at young adult ministry, I would have to become more discerning of when its best to model my beliefs and when it was best to vocalize them. Although both are equally important both are not always necessary. You see, the change I tried to create in them through combating the culture of the "wicked" world ended up resulting in them believing I was harsh and judgmental. However, if I had been able to discern the situation correctly at that time, I could have focused more on modeling the culture of which I claimed so passionately; allowing them to wonder and ask questions. This is the example that Jesus set. Just as much and even more so as Jesus spoke his culture into existence, he modeled it. Counter-culture is not merely bucking the system of the world and telling everyone everything that is wrong and evil and what you are against. Counter-culture is modeling the right behavior with your actions and reinforcing that culture with your words. For us to truly be agents of change in a world of darkness and evil, it is vitally important that we as Christians understand what counter-culture isn't just as much as we understand what kingdom culture is. If we don't, we could end up destroying the very thing we are trying to build.

How We Counter Culture

When considering leaders in the Bible who were masters of living counter-culture, it is nearly impossible not to speak of Daniel. Daniel is such a great example because he represents someone who was completely enslaved into a culture that was wicked and did not serve or honor his God. Being an especially gifted prophet of God and a devout Jew, I am sure that there were moments when he was in a total culture shock. To make it more personal, imagine if America was invaded and you were made a slave, had your name changed and placed in an environment where practically every law and system was the complete opposite of everything you knew. Keeping that thought in mind, consider the details from my past interaction with those young adults at the pool. Just as Daniel was, they are walking into a place where the Lord calls them to forsake their former culture and submit to his lordship, and the systems of the kingdom of God. Furthermore, the precepts and deep things of Christ are far beyond and opposite of anything they have ever known. How do you think they feel? The very thought is insanely overwhelming. I would equate it in most cases as equivalent to trying to describe the color blue to a person who has never seen it. It's a completely different world!

However, in Daniel's case, scripture states he was given the giftings of wisdom in knowledge and skill, in all learning and wisdom. (Daniel 1:17) Daniels trust in God, integrity, and his inner security and confidence in those giftings would serve him well as he navigated the challenges of the culture of captivity. You see in captivity, where Daniel differed from most Christians in today's world was in his approach to finding himself in a new world. This culture or civilization was an OZ that he did not venture to on his own volition, but instead one that found him. So how did a Jewish subject, exhibit one of the greatest examples of counter culture living the world has ever seen? By proving himself through the art of modeling. You see it is not enough to merely speak of culture to those who are foreign. Although speaking and sharing are beneficial, culture can be most effective when it is experienced. Now in reading this, please do not get lost in translation. By no means am I saying Daniel was passive, sin tolerant, or a pushover by remaining relatively silent. I am simply stating that he exercised the gift of wisdom which allowed him to remain relatively silent on what he knew was true until he could model his beliefs.

You see it was the modeling of his culture and the power of God that earned him the trust of the king; then through his gifting, he was promoted above the other wise men. The culmination of wisdom, modeling, and gifting resulted in the introduction and the later growing influence of his culture over the culture of Babylon. Notice Daniel never went around raising cain, starting rebellions, rebuking others or trying to function outside of his grace. He had a silent confidence in God which later allowed his voice the reward of favor and credibility. You may be asking so how do I know when to model and when to speak? Good question. My answer is you must ask for, learn, understand, and practice the gifting of discernment and wisdom. It is the wisdom of the Holy Spirit that will guide you in knowing when to speak and when to model, thus allowing you influence in foreign cultures instead of the appearance of a fool.

Conclusion

Behind every culture is an image. You say really? I say, yes! For example, when you think about what makes America you think of cookouts, sports, rock and roll, theme parks, cowboys, etc. Why? because culture is defined as a way of life and it is culture that creates the image in our mind of how we view the world around us. To be an effective agent of change and further the culture of the kingdom of God on earth one must operate in wisdom and have the gifting and discernment to see beyond the image of power and effectively model the true power of the kingdom. It is the true power of God that proved the God of Daniel true and found the kings' wise men to be foolish. The key is seeing beyond the image and not being captivated or moved by what's around you. Seek God, be faithful to him, model his culture, and opportunities will open for you to make a difference. Remember counter-culture living does not call for Christians to go around beating their chest, telling the world everything they are doing wrong and everything they do or don't agree with. It is modeling the culture the world should be living under and projecting that image to the world, it's the culture of the Kingdom of God that has the power to set free and deliver, we are nothing outside of that culture.

Finally, remember Jesus was a master of living counter-culture. Just as Daniel he lived in a nation that was under the occupational control of another emperor. How did Jesus handle this? Did he go to King Herod and tell him how evil he or the Romans were? Did he go to Pilate and demand that he should repent and set his people free? No. The Bible says that he went about teaching the kingdom and healing the afflicted (Matthew 4:23). Jesus modeled and taught until the influence of his culture was felt and instilled inside 11 future apostles so strongly that they committed to a lifestyle of servitude to him. He then sent them out to model his culture on a larger and grander scale than he did. His culture left an impact and an image of righteousness, peace, and joy; and of purpose hope and love. As followers of Christ, we are called to carry his cross, his culture, and his image. What an honor!!

Keys to Remember:

- We must learn to operate in two worlds.

- You may live in this world, but you are endowed with great power to influence this world with the world to come.

- Living counter-culture shouldn't decrease your effectiveness in this world, it should increase it!

CHAPTER 5

Passing of the Scroll

The unique factors that make up the Daniel gifting proved pivotal to his success very early in his arrival to Babylon. Daniel immediately found favor with the king's chief of eunuchs. Also, through his steadfastness and commitment to stay faithful to God; he witnessed a transition from the servant to a trusted wiseman of the king. It was God's way that would prove most beneficial to the king's objective, ensuring proper nourishment of his new wisemen. As great as this early victory was, this would not be the only manifestation of the power of God in Daniel's life.

Your Gift Will Take You Before Kings

When Daniel appeared within the palace of King Nebuchadnezzar, he was nothing more than a liaison or a failsafe between the Babylonians and the Israelites. It was common practice in those times for kings who conquered foreign lands to retain individuals of that land to help with cultural relations communication barriers, keeping the peace and avoiding rebellions. However, one day King Nebuchadnezzar had a dream that was so troubling that he could not sleep (Daniel 2:1). He called for all his magicians, astrologers, sorcerers, and Chaldeans in hopes that they could tell him the meaning of his dream. He informed them all that if they could not tell him the meaning of his dream that he would cut them and their families into pieces. However, he stated that if they could interpret the dreams, they would receive gifts, rewards, and great honor. The king, knowing that they would seek time to conjure a lie informed them that they must answer the dream immediately. The wise men listened to the dream and after hearing the king's dream shook in fear as they were unable to provide a meaning of the dream. King Nebuchadnezzar then ordered that all the wise men be killed including Daniel (Daniel 2:1-14).

In an effort to save not only his life but the lives of the other wise men, Daniel speaks to the Captain of the king's guard and asks that he ask the king for time to provide the interpretation for his dream. The secret was then revealed to Daniel in a dream. After receiving the interpretation of the dream from God, Daniel offers an incredible praise of thanksgiving to God acknowledging his great power and accepting the gift of wisdom and discernment of which God had given him (Daniel 2: 20-23). Daniel full of faith, then went before King Nebuchadnezzar and interpreted the meaning of the troubling image from his dream. After Daniels' interpretation, King Nebuchadnezzar fell to his face before Daniel and commanded that he receive offerings and burnt incense. However, the most incredible aspect of the whole passage is the acknowledgment of the one true God by the king. Once he collected himself, the king stated that Daniels God was, in fact, the one true God the king of kings. Furthermore, he stated that God was the revealer of secrets. A fact that will prove true more and more during Daniel's captivity. Finally, the king gave Daniel lavish gifts and promoted him to rule over the whole province of Babylon and chief of all the wise men. After receiving his promotion Daniel then promoted Shadrach, Meshach, and Abed-Nego. This passage not only shows the purpose of gifting (to give God glory) but also the power of gifting. Daniel and his Godly companions went from mere slaves to the rulers of their captives. They remained faithful and separated unto God, and God showed himself faithful to them in such a way that even an imperialistic king had to acknowledge the power of the one true living God.

In life, it is very easy to feel as if we are just average and that there is nothing special about us. However, there is an unmeasurable amount of greatness on the inside of you. God has placed gifts inside that will take you in the presence of politicians, Presidents, CEOs and yes, even Kings. However, you must understand that there is a process of walking in these endowments. That cost is consecration and separation before God, and the development of a prayer life. These practices will allow us to hear such secrets as well as the voice of God concerning the direction and the use of our giftings. As Christians, we serve a God of results. God has a will, a purpose, and a timing. The synchronization of these three things bring about miraculous results. If there are times that you feel powerless, or ineffective in life, ask yourself: am I in God's will, purpose, and timing? Pray as Daniel did then most importantly listen for God's voice. It is then that you will find his direction and the moment for the application of the gift will present itself allowing you to receive powerful results!! It is never a matter of if God gave you and gifts? It is simply understanding how to recognize and respond to the gifting. God has always and still to this day gives liberally to those who ask. In fact, the wisdom, understanding, and discernment he gave to Daniel were so deep and immeasurable that Daniel was able to see into worlds that he would never live in! Should you choose to read deeper into the life of Daniel you will find that this would not be the only time his gift of discernment was used to interpret a vision or dream. Furthermore, his first promotion would not be his last. Nebuchadnezzar would soon lose his thrown and the kingdom of his son would be overthrown by Darius King of the Medes. Daniel, as he was for King Nebuchadnezzar, would stand in the courts of yet another captor of which he would be used to influence. But it was during this era of captivity that his gifting would reach its heights.

Seeing in Two Worlds

During the reign of King Darius, (the Mede) Daniel began having visions that went far beyond anything he had ever seen or dreamed before. The Lord began gifting Daniel with visions of the collapse of kingdoms and the rise of empires. In Chapters 11&12 specifically, he beings to see the times of the end and prophecies his recollection. In these visions, Daniel would see and write things concerning wars, the rapture of the church, the anti-Christ, and just up to the events of the tribulation. In fact, Daniel saw so far into the future that he saw a time of which I believe we are living today. Daniels revelation in these visions was at such a point that Michael the Arc Angel informed him to shut up the words and seal the book until the time of the end when many shall run to and from and knowledge would increase. Daniel was so overtaken by what he saw he could only ask, "When will these things happen"? However, the angel told Daniel to go his way until the end and that he would take his allotted place at the end of days (Daniel 12:1-13).

Passing of the Scroll

What really captivates me about this passage is the manner by which such things were revealed to Daniel. What would motivate God to allow Daniel to receive such revelation exceeding way beyond his time? The revelation and understanding were so far beyond Daniels' time that for the first time in his life he says, "I could not understand it" (Daniel 12:8). I believe that Daniel could not understand what he saw in the vision because what he witnessed were events that occur in a world millenniums beyond that of his own. In (Daniel 12:4) Daniel is instructed to shut up the words and seal the scroll until the time of the end where many shall run to and from, and knowledge should increase. It was for this new world that this word would apply to and not the world for which Daniel was living. This would be a future world where people are flying, taking trains, planes, and communicating in ways that Daniel literally could not understand or comprehend it.

It may be easy to think, well that's just your interpretation of this passage. My response would be, that's very true. However, I would also ask you to consider the passing of the scroll. In the book of Revelation Chapter 10, the apostle John has an incredible encounter with God concerning the times of the end. In his vision, the angel appeared with a little scroll in his hand. Then a voice from heaven told John, "go and take the scroll from the hand of the angel who is standing on the sea and the land". John went to the angel and told the angel, give me the scroll". The angel then replied, "take and eat". John took the scroll and ate it. In his mouth, it was sweet as honey, but it made his stomach bitter. John was then told, "you must again prophesy about many peoples, nations, languages, and kings" (Revelation 10:5-11).

To clarify, we are still talking about Daniel, but I would be doing you a complete injustice not to address this incredible connection between Daniel and the apostle John. Furthermore, this passage solidifies the truth of the extent of Daniel's gifting and just how powerful and outside of his world, his gifting was. After Daniel has his vision of the end times, the angel told him to shut up and seal the words until the time of the end. I want to direct your attention towards (Daniel 12:6) in this passage. The location of the angel was above the waters of the stream. Now fast forward hundreds of years later the same angel in the same location as he was with Daniel, now hands the apostle John the scroll to eat. John then begins to write the vision of the end from where Daniel left off hundreds of years before him. Wow! There is so much more to visions that God gave Daniel. I would love to expound upon them, however, that is not the purpose or intent of this book. I do encourage you to go back and read them for more in-depth understanding.

Gifting Beyond What You Can Imagine

The story of Daniel and his journey of captivity is nothing short of incredible. His gifting allowed him to be an anomaly in a culture whose world system was built on images, vanity, and idolatry. One of the marquee aspects that I want you to take away is that his trust in God and understanding of his gifting play a pivotal part in his accession from a captive, to wisemen, to head of the wise men in a culture that did not honor his God. That in itself is a miracle! However, it does not stop there. God gave Daniel such a measure of gifting and discernment that he was able to not only understand interpret the dreams of kings, but he was also able to see thousands of years into the future; into the days we are currently living in! That is the measure of which God gifted to Daniel, the gifting was above all he could ever imagine it being.

Even today God is currently seeking believers who will stand boldly, grounded in their faith amid a culture of which many people do not reverence or honor him. Furthermore, he is seeking to reveal and unlock inside of us a gifting that will allow us to see and discern the secret things which are to come but also the hidden of hurts of the lost and unsaved. The Lord is seeking believers whose hearts are pure and turned towards him, who care, love, and seek to impact this next generation in a mighty way. It is these people to which God has and will impart such overwhelming power, on a wide-scale basis, and in a mighty way! How do you access this power you ask? Through a willing and pure heart. The times we are living in require the ability to see and discern like never before. Ask God to reveal the mysteries to you and pray for a trained and obedient spirit. I believe that by doing this you will receive a measure of gifting beyond anything you could ever imagine!

Conclusion

The passing of the scrolls is one of the most intriguing occurrences in the entire Bible. It is a representation of a truth which transcends, the sands of time. First Daniel receives a revelation beyond his time, John then picks up the scroll and continues the completion of the revelation which started with Daniel. The level of understanding and discernment was both beyond their time and anything they both could ever imagine. Although there is nothing that can be added to or taken away from this revelation; there is still an abundance of mysteries in which the lord is seeking to reveal to those who are found faithful towards him. The Prophet Joel prophesied in the last days that God would pour out his spirit upon all flesh, that the sons and daughters would prophesy, and old men should have visions and dreams (Joel 2:28). This tells us that there are many more mysteries left to be revealed, and many more dreams and visions to be interpreted. Just as we saw with Daniel, this gift of discerning of mysteries will be the catalyst to revolutionize this culture and show them the incredible power of God! The maker of all heaven and earth, who dwelled before, in and, soon to be after time is still a God who reveals the secrets and mysteries of the kingdom. He is and will continue to give this gifting in such a manner above that which we can imagine. Question is, do you receive it? And are you ready!?

Keys to Remember:

- God is a God of abundance, when he gives, he gives beyond what you can imagine.

- There are levels of discernment and understanding that empower you to see in two worlds.

- The passing of the scrolls between Daniel and John signifies that the gifting of dreams, visions, and the discernment of mysteries is timeless.

- Though nothing can be added to or taken away from prophecy, we still operate in time and within that time there are secrets and mysteries which are revealed to believers daily. The revealing of these mysteries are faith builders which will serve to draw people towards a powerful and loving God.

- We are living in the days of which the spirit of God is moving mightily on the sons and daughters of God. Prepare dream, revelation, and prophetic words and be obedient to the voice of the Holy Spirit.

CHAPTER 6

Modern Day Babylon

Though the glory of Babylon has long passed, the correlations between the culture of Babylon and that of today's world are undeniable. Today, we are seeing a widescale resurrection of a culture of which many people have forgotten or turned away from God. Because of this, the rise of greed, power, lust, and pleasure has increased. In (2 Timothy 3:1-2) the apostle Paul wrote to Timothy that in the last days perilous times will come: for many will be lovers of themselves, lovers of money, boasters, proud, blasphemers, disobedient to parents, unthankful, unholy, unloving, unforgiving, slanderers, without self-control, brutal, despisers of good, traitors, headstrong, haughty, lovers of pleasure rather than God, having a form of Godliness but denying the power.

When I read these scriptures, it is hard for me not to cringe. At times it can even make me feel, what's the use in trying if the world is doomed for its own self-destruction? It is not my intent to be pessimistic or negative in any way but if you are not aware of the time and seasons, we are living in allow me to be your personal Paul Revere and to inform you the enemy is coming.

Satan is active and working in every realm imaginable. Politically, social, relationally, economically, globally, and even in the body of Christ. There is no avenue of which Satan is not seeking to attack. The most intriguing aspect of the manner of his attack is how he continually uses the image to blind and deceive the inhabitants of the world. Satan has been and even today is lurking the earth as a roaring lion seeking whoever he can devour. Just as Satan used something as simple as an apple to bring about the fall of man; he is now using the very things we desire (even good things) as a way to draw us into the culture of this world. As Christians we are not exempt, now more than ever is the time for us to wake up and take our position. We truly are at war. However, our war is not against flesh and blood as such is with a carnal war; our war is a war for the souls of mankind. For the lost, for the deceived, for the hurt and the broken. It's time for us as believers to recognize and take action.

War on Every Front

In the books of Daniel and Revelation, when speaking of the end times both authors write that in the days of the end, war will be made on the saints in an attempt to wear us down. As someone who is a believer in the fact that we are currently in what the Bible would call the "last days", I believe now is that time. Currently, like never before Christians are waking up daily in a world that is constantly shifting more and more to into something we can no longer recognize. Agendas both politically and socially are being pushed that have ostracized believers into labels such as intolerant, unloving, and judgmental. The Christian foundation of our culture is under a blitzkrieg from the kingdom of darkness.

OZ and the End Time Delusion

In 2 Thessalonians 2: 10-11 Paul writes of the deception that will run rapid in the times of the end. Many will be deceived by false truth and become entrenched in lying wonders. For this reason, Paul writes God will send them a strong delusion that they should believe the lie, that they may all be condemned who did not believe the truth but had pleasure in unrighteousness (v.11). If this scripture is read incorrectly it could be that interpreted that God is sending a delusion to good people that is causing them to be deceived. However, that is not the case. The truth is a delusion is a high level of confusion. There are steps before arriving at delusion; the first being a thought. Once these thoughts are pondered on and acted upon over time, they become deeply grounded in us. It as this moment that a person ultimately deceives him or herself. So, in this passage, the true interpretation is that the people have become so strongly entrenched in their beliefs that there is no going back, they have become reprobate and thus are headed towards destruction.

This is the ultimate purpose of the OZ effect. To present to you any and everything created by God in a perverted manner but cloaked with the appearance of truth, love and acceptance. The scripture mentions lying wonders, and miracles because the Oz of this world or Satan understands that every good and effective lie has a form of truth. For this reason, Satan begins all of his engagement and activities as an angel of light. This is what makes his images so appealing. In picking his targets, no one is off-limits, not even professing believers.

Delusion of Love

One of the greatest delusions being used in the days we are living in is the delusion of love. I believe Satan is most effective in this is because it's something we all want and desire. Also, it's something that can be used to tie the hands of believers, with rebuttals like, well isn't God a God of love. Because of this subtle deceit, many are forsaking the sanctity of marriage between a man and a woman and have instead taken up homosexual relationships. However, what many homosexuals don't understand is that in these relationships, although some form of love does exist; the relationships do not have the ability to bring forth life; in other words, they are fruitless and cannot bring about the multiplication of population which

God commanded. Furthermore, many same-sex couples fall into a delusion that everyone who does not believe in their relationship is against them; thus, falling deeper and deeper into deception. Once the deception reaches the level of delusion, we then see men and women having sex changes. This is a representation of being so involved in a lifestyle in which there is no relative thought at that moment of repentance. Once gender roles and identity are confused the world is then plunged further and further into deception. Just as the Bible says, brother will stand against brother and sister against sister. Sadly, we are seeing this happen not only in the United States but all over the world.

One of the most unfortunate aspects regarding this is the issue that many individuals involved in same-sex couples are people who have been hurt, abused, molested, or have witnessed failed marriage after failed marriage. In some very sad and severe cases the molestation was from someone of the same sex resulting in the child being confused about their sexualality due to the nature of their first sexual experience. It is at that point that many begin to give up on love, viewing their homosexual relationship as either normal, or a stand against the oppression of men or the expectations and norms of society.

Note: I will address this subject more towards the end, but if you are reading this book and you are struggling with homosexually please don't take this as a judgment against

you. I want you to know that you are loved, and I have a personal word for you that will inspire hope in you.

The Delusion of Human Rights

When I grew up learning of human rights, I learned about Abraham Lincoln, Martin Luther King, Mother Theresa, and Nelson Mandela. Today as our kids are taught human rights, their subjects are pro-choice and pro-life. When I consider the stance and lives of the heroes mentioned above it is hard to imagine them marching and protest for freedom that would in any way deny the freedom of others. Doing so would make them hypocritical at best. However, presently there is a strong humanistic deception growing ever so popular that influences men and women to believe that it is civil and just to terminate the life of an unborn child. To make it a bit plainer, some people celebrate Martin Luther King for advocating for freedom and liberty for all; and then turn around and advocate for the termination of the unborn. It is important that you understand there are multiple aspects of belief concerning abortion. Some believe in full out termination even up to birth, and then others who believe in termination up to a certain point. One of the main arguments in the defense of this practice is it is my body; I can do what I want. However, once a woman becomes pregnant, she now has two bodies, one which does not belong to her.

I have watched several interviews regarding abortion and one of the things I hear most often is, if a woman is out "having fun" and gets pregnant, she shouldn't have to choose between a baby and her career. It is statements like these that reveal the true heart behind the image of this delusion. The history of abortion goes back way before the 19th century. In fact, the Bible is full of accounts of child sacrifice and murder, from the killing of babies by Pharaoh, sacrificing of children to Moloch, and even the killing of babies by king Herod in an attempt to find and kill baby Jesus. Note, that all of these were done in an attempt to gain or protect monetary gain or power. It is all humanistic in nature and places the desires of comfort and pleasure over the blood of innocence. This is a complete perversion of human rights. It allows people to believe they have the freedom to take the freedom of the innocent.

> *Note: I will address this subject more towards the end of this book but if you are reading this book and you are struggling with guilt over an abortion please don't take this as a judgment against you. I want you to know that you are loved, and I have a personal word for you that will inspire hope in you.*

Delusion of the Church

Before ever addressing the evils which would be present in the world in these last days; the first people the Apostle John addressed was the 7 churches (Revelation

Chapter 1-3). I believe it is due to the fact that judgment always has and always will begin with the house of God.

"For it is time that judgment must begin with the house of God: and if it first begins at us, what shall be the outcome for them that obey not the gospel of God?" (1 Peter 4:17)

As the church, we are called to be light and salt. Yet just as John wrote concerning this matter in Revelation, much of the church has become lukewarm. We have become comfortable with hyper-grace teaching, a 20-minute sermon, and a worship concert on Sunday morning. Many of us then go to work on Monday and complain about how wicked the world is yet do nothing to light the world or bring it flavor. Many of us have ourselves become delusional and Oz'd into believing that everything is ok and that we must merely hold on until Jesus comes back. Brothers and sisters, this is so far from the truth. If Jesus is our first love, then our relationship with him should be reflected in the way in we influence the world around us. This was demonstrated in Jesus' relationship with God the father when he stated, "I have come down from heaven to do the will of my father who sent me" (John 6:38). Jesus didn't walk the earth to merely exist and die, he was a man on a mission. Today much of the church has become satisfied and comfortable. We spiritualize our own will and remain powerless and ineffective and then we wonder why God's presence is not present in our workplaces. Furthermore, we have fallen into a delusion that the world is supposed to come to us, when in fact we were told to go into the world. The church has become a safe place for the stubborn and comfortable. That is why John addressed the church first. If we don't get it right, then how can we expect the world to get it right? It's time for us to wake up, and that is what the Lord is raising up the Daniel remnant to do.

Conclusion

The intention of this is not to be negative, but to provide a brief and accurate assessment concerning the state of the world's culture. Matthew 24:37-39 states that as the days of Noah were, so shall the coming of the son of man be. Please understand these were the times in which there was so much wickedness on the Earth that God flooded the world. There is absolutely no doubt that we are living of which Daniel and John prophesied as the time of the end. These times are signified by the rise of wickedness, hate, lust, greed, pride, self-exaltation and a confusion and delusion so strong that even believers are being deceived. Futhermore, the times are plagued with the images which draw in many, only to lead them into fatal deception. Though these things remain prevalent, even more so prevalent is the fact that God is pouring out his spirit on his sons and daughter (Joel 2:32). God is unleashing a powerful anointing on believers all over the world. An anointing that bears the discernment needed to see beyond the image of what appears right and can lead others towards truth. An anointing which bears the heart of compassion. An anointing which does not ridicule, judge, or belittle; but instead listens, discerns, and provides interpretations which shed light to outshine the confusion and the darkness in this world. The time is now that the remnant will rage war against the Oz's of our modern-day Babylon.

Keys to Remember:

- We are now living in days of Noah, in a time in which wickedness is at an all-time high.

- We must avoid deception at all costs. A little deception can lead to delusion.

- As the church, we cannot be satisfied with merely existing we must be light and salt.

- If we are lukewarm, we cannot be the solution to the wickedness of this world.

- There is a remnant rising with a Daniel gifting. They will operate with compassion and will stand for God amid wickedness. They will change culture with grace and love and lead the lost out of the darkness.

CHAPTER 7

The War on Truth and Sincerity

One of the unique aspects of Paul's writings was his commitment to truth and sincerity when bringing correction or exhortation. When addressing the church of Corinth Paul writes regarding the Christian customs, "Therefore let us celebrate the feast, not with the old leaven of leaven of malice, but with the unleavened bread of sincerity and truth" (1 Corinthians 5:8). There are days where I have read 1 Corinthians 10-15 times and this scripture had always intrigued me regarding its meaning. However, as I began to write this book it became much clearer. The church of Corinth was known for its great works and spiritual gifts, however, there were many contentions among them regarding the operations of the church. Among these issues were strife, comparison, and pride.

Throughout the content of his letters, Paul addresses these issues in order to bring correction and establish order to bring more effectiveness to their community. It is the tone he sets in 1 Corinthians chapter 1 and two keywords which led me to the conclusion much of what he was addressing was the manner of which they went about doing right. Notice in the scripture mentioned above Paul wrote celebrating not with the leaven of malice. Malice is a word of dissension. He then says instead let us celebrate with the unleavened bread of truth and sincerity. It appears, what is he speaking of is in concerning celebration. Reading the scripture in context leads me to believe he is addressing the manner in which Christians relate to each other.

The War on Truth

Today's culture has found itself in a massive war on truth. This war, however, is unilateral or one could even say asymmetric. Currently, the world is at odds about one major issue; what is truth? To every person, this can be different and that's what makes the war so asymmetric. Somewhere in between the views and ideas of others, lies absolute truth; or what theologist might call infallible truth. In between that also lie countless arguments, debates, disagreements, indifference and even at times even hate. So how do we know who is right? If everyone believes their viewpoint is right, who and what decides what right? Scripture plainly states that there will be a day where all will come to the knowledge of Christ. That means when all is said and done, the truth will be made known to all and proven true. However, on earth, we are tasked with sharing to the truth with a world in which many of the inhabitants believe in any and everything from other Gods, Scientology Atheism, and a plethora of other things. So, where amid such difference can we find a bridge? It is the chasm between the asymmetric balance of truth which results in many casualties. These casualties range from broken marriages, lost friendships, and even loss of life.

What makes it harder to combat is that with the rise of democracies from that of empires and autocracies in previous centuries throughout civilization; individuals have now been given power like never before to share their beliefs with high levels of public visibility. With technology like Facebook, YouTube and other social media platforms it's no longer broad spectrum of ideological difference such as with the Lutherans and the Catholics, and the Christians and Islamics. Truth has now become more polarized on a level we have never seen before.

I can remember my first year at Marion Military Institute. At the time Barrack Obama was running against John McCain and Sarah Palin. One day in the chow hall 2 cadets became engaged in a political debate. I was a new cadet at the time and tried my hardest to stay out of it, but the zeal and pride inside of me, especially at the age of 19, would not allow me to sit in silence. I began to combat the Obama supporters and soon what began as a conversation quickly became dissension. Several of those people would never speak to me again both at Marion, after graduation, and even to this day. Although at the time it seemed right to me to stand up to what I believed to be the truth. At that point, we were all relative strangers. They had not even had the chance to know me personally. They knew everything I was for and against and that I was determined to be right. But what did that truly accomplish? Furthermore, fast forward ten years later and examine the aftereffects of that conversation. I am on fire for God, full of the word, and much more mature naturally and spiritually. However, those individuals do not see that, they remember a prideful, obnoxious, young kid who was determined to be right; thus, to this day they find me distasteful. I have little to no witness with them. This is a perfect example of people who have fallen in the chasm or divide between truths. Eventually, I had to learn that proving a point is not worth the sacrificing of a relationship. In order to be effective with sharing my views with other people, I would need to find the bridge; I would need to end my war on truth.

A Church at War

As I shared in the counter-culture chapter of this book, some of the behaviors I took concerning truth, were a result of my natural and spiritual upbringing. It was great that I was taught truth, but I didn't know how to be effective with truth. There is an old saying that goes, the truth hurts. How true that can be. The truth when mishandled or in the wrong hands can become a weapon. As confusing as this can be for some, it is no less true. A gun in the home of a family can be for protection, but in the hand of someone with wrong intentions, the view of it becomes altered. It is important that we as Christians are responsible with truth, meaning we are not intentionally using the truth as the means to control the unwilling or unknowingly using it be right, it is at this moment the truth loses its ability to be effective through us.

As a young adult minister, I was very active on Sam Houston State University Campus. Truthfully, it was one of my favorite aspects of young adult ministry. I will also add it was a chance to demonstrate my repentance concerning past mishandlings of truth from my past. As I walked on Campus, I would see people from different ministries with tables set up in front of the student center. At these tables there was everything for Mormons to Baptist Student Ministry students, sharing their beliefs with any and everyone who would listen. In one instance, I ran across a crowd of people who had surrounded a group of people creaming on a microphone and holding signs. The signs were concerning the issues of abortion and homosexual marriage in addition to signs regarding judgment and hell. As I walked closer, I was able to make out the words of the gentlemen on the microphone. He was speaking to some young ladies who appeared to be of same-sex relationship and was publicly confronting them with questions and attacks towards their lifestyle. The two ladies' faces were completely red and many of the students began yelling and cussing.

I then asked myself, what is this guy really accomplishing? It is sad because most of what he was saying I agreed with as sound doctrine. However, the method of publicly shaming these young ladies was only bringing out embarrassment and outrage. At that moment something rose inside of me and I began telling the people that God loved them and that this was not his way. Several students turned towards me and began talking to me and I was able to encourage them and invite them to college service. When I look back at the actions of those Christians that day, it's hard not to feel both shame and sympathy. In everything they were doing to share truth, nothing was accomplished, and no one was won to the kingdom. The chasm remained unbridged thus they were simply at war with the truth.

The Bridge of Sincerity

One of our many roles and probably one of the most important is the role of ambassador. An ambassador is one who represents his or her country in dealings or negotiations with that of another in which a resolution to difference may need resolution. Christ calls us to be ambassadors which means we are direct representatives of his kingdom. When people see us, they see Christ. How we conduct ourselves in meetings and at the negotiation table will either push us towards peace or further the gap between us and the world. During a conflict between two sides, the actors must first come to the conclusion that they do not want conflict. This means leaving ego and pride at the door and bring sincerity and understanding to the forefront. This is the only way in which two sides at odds will be able to work towards an agreement or understanding without further conflict. As ambassadors, we are to avoid conflict if at all possible. Ambassadors are not sent to set fires or fan flames. We are to be masters at bridge-building and deal with all conflict through prayer and navigate conflict through the eyes of love, mercy, and grace. To approach the table without these components is unauthorized engagement.

I have several friends who operate in the area of street ministry. In their ministry, they go to bars, sports arenas, concert venues, etc.., and yell the gospel to people. I have watched several of their videos and am grieved every time. During their nights of ministry, they are threatened, spat at, cursed out and ridiculed. As all this chaos occurs one of them is usually videoing everything going on. I have even heard them call out these people as demon-possessed and wicked on video. Unfortunately, it seems these men also view themselves as martyrs for the faith, and some may view them in that light. However, in everything they have done, I have yet to see or hear about one victory. It is always everyone is evil, no one wants to receive Jesus. Yet the Bible says the harvest is plentiful and the laborers are few! What if their methods are ineffective and maybe the people that are lashing out feel targeted and violated instead of loved? What if they feel sincerity is not at the table? What if they are not rejecting Jesus, but instead rejecting what they believe to an attack from the insincere?

When Jesus walked the earth, he clearly stated that he did not come to the world to condemn the world but that through him the world might be saved. Furthermore, he solidified his words with his actions with all who met him. Specifically, I recall his dealing with the woman at the well. Notice that nowhere in the Bible did Jesus go to where sinners frequented and demand that they repent. On the contrary, he met such people incidentally and led by the Holy Spirit inside of him was always able to give the portion that they needed. For the woman at the well; she was thirsty for something to fulfill her that she could not find in the world or in the many men for which she kept company. Jesus identified her issues gracefully and provided her with a portion of water in which she would never thirst again. Even after revealing her sin to her she was impacted by her visit with Jesus that she became an evangelist of sorts as she went to the city and proclaimed come and see the man who told me everything that I have ever done (John 4:7-30). Notice Jesus was effective because he showed sincere individual love and concern for this woman. He did not reveal truth to her to show off, or be right, but to set her free. The sole intention of the truth is to set people free. For this reason, there can be no additives or leaven to the bread of truth. For it to be most effective it must be pure. It must be free of ego, pride, and vanity. Once this is achieved, we will see more people set free by the truth of the Gospel of Jesus Christ.

Walking in Sincerity

One of the saddest truths in the body of Christ is that much of the world including young believers have taken the position that many Christians are fake. In (Matthew 5:13) Jesus states, "you are the salt of the earth; but if the salt loses its flavor, how shall it be seasoned? It is then good for nothing but to be thrown out and trampled underfoot by men." In my years of service to the body of Christ, I can recall on multiple occasions well-meaning church people making blanket statements regarding the condition of the world. They are so wicked, they are sick, these people are disgusting, etc. Though these things may be true, one of the things I find intriguing is the fact that the world is doing their job. Scripture tells us that sin would be increased on the earth during the times of the end. My question is, are we as Christians doing our jobs? Are we living counter-culture?

As Christians, I believe we fall into thought fallacies often. We constantly use clichés and say things like, the resurrection power is on the inside of me. Yet the power in many of us lies dormant. This is why the world is not to our taste, or you could say we don't care for the flavor. To truly be salt and light we must walk in the truth. Clichés will not work, excellence of speech will not work, for the world to be properly seasoned we must demonstrate our walks with the power which we claim. Also, we must add to that truth understanding and sincerity, this allows the people we are addressing to digest what we are saying so the seed of the word can take life into their spirit.

Where We Have Missed It

As previously stated, we as Christians must ensure that we demonstrate care and love before planting seeds. This is no different than a gardener who tills the ground before planting tomato seeds. The tilled soil will provide the seed with the best chance to grow properly. Where many Christians fail today, are in their dealings with the controversial areas of today.

I previously discussed that there is much more to the rise of homosexuality than what meets the eyes. In no way is what I write next a justification or a stamp of approval to these actions. However, it is my hope that it challenges believers to really be spirit-led, in their dealings with people who deal with their sexual orientation and identities. Many people have been bullied, mentally abused, molested, raped, or have experienced other forms of trauma regarding relationships during their lives. For this many become disorientated, angry, and hurt to such a point that it alters their perspective regarding love and relationship. Sadly, because of many of our upbringings, many Christians run guns a blazing ready to shoot truth bombs and tell them all about how what they are doing is sin and how they are going to hell. We view ourselves as some John the Baptist, or maybe a revolutionary for Christ. However, in all reality when we are on Facebook speaking how disgusting and vile they are, or how they are going to hell, we really look foolish. That is because we have not been taught and properly trained on how to uproot and build. We only know how to pull up or tear-out. Many of us are image-driven thus when we people we want to trim them so that they will look how we expect them to look naturally. Every day we bring our Jesus clippers and go to snipping away at people.

If you have ever clipped or trimmed hedges you know that this just results in more growth. However, maturity and sincerity take time to understand the roots. It speaks healing to the molestation, the rejection and the pain they feel. When you understand the roots, you understand the true source of bondage. To understand the root is to be spirit-led, to only judge by appearance is to be led by sight or by the flesh. You cannot judge the fruit of an unbeliever (that is only applicable to believers as unbelievers cannot bear the fruits of the Holy Spirit). So, what are we doing when we clip them? we are solidifying the notion that we are judgmental hypocrites. This is not living counter-culture.

True sincerity will always approach the lost and dying with the truth directed at the root. That because they are led internally and have taken the time privately to exercise their understanding through the reading of God's word and prayer. When we approach the sinner to understand how they became involved in this lifestyle whatever the sin maybe we show them that we care. Once they know we care, they are more likely to expose their roots or share their stories. From there we can see properly the roots, and strongholds which need to be torn out and down and can plant new seeds of truth in their life. Could you still be rejected? Yes, however, I would rather be rejected and respected, than be rejected and have misrepresented Christ.

It is important that we understand the principles of applying truth in the world we are living in. We must not let political allegiance and ideology blind us from our mission of ambassadorship. There are women who are tormented at night because of past abortions. A choice at 16 made from fear should not define them for life, better yet after they are saved. They do not need to be told that they are murders on social media. What they need to hear is that they are forgiven for their sin and washed clean and empowered to teach other ladies the same thing. This is not pacifying or accepting sin. This is walking in truth and sincerity, treating people as the individuals they are and not polarizing them or pushing them into isolation.

Conclusion

In the culture of today's world is not enough to merely speak the truth, we must add to it love, grace, and sincerity. What we fail to understand is that the culture of darkness is nothing like the culture of heaven. There is a huge divide between the two. A bridge must be made between these two worlds and that bridge is a man. That man's name is Jesus Christ who died to bridge the chasm between God and man. It is now our job to represent Jesus as his ambassadors and walk the lost across the bridge; out of the darkness and into the marvelous light. Because of the nature of this mission, we must use wisdom and be spirit led. You wouldn't go to China and yell at people and be mad because they didn't understand you right? No. Because the culture is completely different, they speak a completely different language. The same principle applies to spiritually. We cannot as ambassadors yell at and belittle people because they don't look or act how we expect them. They are unsaved! They are supposed to sin! To be effective in living counter-culture we must utilize the interpreter, that interpreter is the all-knowing all power Holy Spirit, who draws all mankind to the love and powerful God of the universe. To properly reflect his culture, we must ensure that we bear his heart and his wisdom in our dealings with the lost. This is what it means to live counter-culture.

Keys to Remember:

- As Christians, we are to deal with each other with truth and sincerity.

- Sincerity is the bridge between the gap of what we and others believe to be truth. Without sincerity, common ground is not possible.

- As Christians, we are called to be ambassadors "peacemakers". This doesn't mean compromising the truth but instead taking the time to sit at the table of understanding.

- In order to change culture, we must approach people from the inside out and not the outside in as Jesus did.

- Counter culture is not isolationism or polarization, it is taking the time to understand people and to add your measure of salt and flavor to their life.

Protecting Your Identity

One of the best ways for us to live a counter-culture lifestyle is to protect our identity. Not identity in terms of our social security number, or our looks. But our identity concerning the unique gifts, interests, talents, and abilities God has placed inside of us. Our identity is our spiritual DNA, our make-up which determines how we will look, talk, and even our dictates our mannerisms. What's even crazier is that our spiritual identity is even tied to our destiny. Remember Jeremiah.

God personally tells Jeremiah before he was formed in his mother's womb, he set apart, appointed, and called to be a prophet to the nations (Jeremiah 1:5). This tells us that everything Jeremiah needed to be what God called him to be was already inside of him. Many of us just like Jeremiah can have moments in life where we question our purpose and existence and maybe wonder how we fit. We feel like we have to find something we don't have so we go wondering place to place to and from seeking people places and things we think can show us who we are and where we need to be; just as Dorothy and her companions did in the Wizard of Oz. However, when succumbing to such practices, we wander deeper and deeper into the void, thus growing further away from our true identity thus resulting in a feelings of insecurity, and hopelessness.

Idols, Insecurity, and the Image

It is an unfortunate fact that in today's culture most anything and everyone has the potential to become an Oz. This has become such an epidemic that it can even be done unintentionally. In determining the cause of such an epidemic, one of the leading factors of the Oz epidemic in culture comes from the sin of idolatry. Recalling once more the life of Daniel in the city of Babylon. King Nebuchadnezzar had an image built from gold in which all people were to bow down and worship. As cliché as we can be with the repetition of scripture, have you ever thought what would make people bow down to something made of gold? What made the people worship objects of clay, bronze, wood, gold, etc.? I believe that it's the result of insecurity inside of these individuals. An insecurity that seeks the existence of something much larger and much greater than themselves. Notice, that there is much truth to this. However, that great thing is not the Oz which the king created; it was the one true God.

American culture has taken center stage as the epitome of idolatry. Many actors, musicians, and celebrities are given terms such as Icon, Idols, and yes even God's. Many of the youth and young adults of the culture grow up listening to and watching the examples of these public figures. They see the image of fame, the lights, money, cars and immediately begin to exalt these people into positions of power and influence in their lives. Our young people verbally call them their idols and watch shows which program their minds to believe these people are something they aren't and to have this power and influence they need to be like these people.

Consequently, our young people, as Dorothy did, begin to see their world around them as boring, empty, and mundane. They begin to become vain in their imagination and desire the life of another. It is at this moment that insecurity with their true identity begins and they trade their identity for the image of what will give them power and meaning in life. We must end the idolatry in America if we are to end the insecurity in our young people. An image or an Oz should never cause you to doubt who you are. That's why as Daniel did, we must learn to see and discern the images of culture in their proper perspective.

Idolatry in the Church

One of the strangest things about idolatry is that it doesn't always manifest in an obvious way. Sometimes in life, we have mentors, friends, teachers, and pastors in which we may look up to and esteem highly. Although this is great and honorable, there must be a balance to such esteem. In the church today there we have seen a drastic rise in the number of what I would call "cookie-cutter" Christians. I believe the word epidemic has now become suitable. For years we have been affected by the concept that every minister must have the same message, personality, style, anointing, and charisma. However, this is far from the truth. God is a God of creativity and diversity. He does not create copies or clones. Although anointings can be transferred it does not mean that another personality and individual traits can be transferred. God designs us to be different to be unique. Your uniqueness is what aids you in your purpose. It works hand in hand with your identity.

When the rise of the unorthodox ministers began in the early-mid 2000s, the world saw the stereotypical pastors and evangelist in 3-piece suits become skinny jean wearing, blue jean jacket wearing rock stars. In no way do I mean to criticize, I find it rather cool and unrestrictive. However, what I noticed is that along with the charismatic cultural shift, came a fashion-obsessed, identity stealing form of obsession. What was meant to make the worldly and unsaved entering the church feel less focused on dress code and more comfortable, soon became the template for the cookie-cutter Christian leader factory. Over time the epidemic would extend beyond clothes. Young ministers and pastors would begin to emulate the pioneers of this new age Christian persona. They began to adopt the way they communicated, the way they styled their hair, even the way they pointed to the camera in promotional videos and other visible mannerisms.

When Paul told young Timothy to follow me as I follow Christ, he did not mean dress how I dress, adopt my mannerisms, my interests, and my personality. He meant to follow my example, conduct, and devotion to the things of God. Because this has become so misunderstood, young people seeking to be trained and discipled for ministry believe that means adopting another life, another image, and another persona opposite of the one God has given them. Your identity is linked to your purpose. To abandon your identity is to abandon your purpose. You cannot walk in the fullness of your destiny with an altered identity.

Saul's Armor

The story of David is rather intriguing in that it depicts the possibility of the simple and humble being projected into incredible heights. David was a young Shepherd, who was the forgotten of his fathers' children until the day he was anointed to be the next king. Although his father and brothers did not think much of him David was a skilled Shepherd. It was during this time which he mastered the use of his sling in the defense of his sheep from the bear and the lion. These tests built his confidence and understand in his identity. His family saw him as a mere Shepherd boy, but David saw himself as a warrior. One day a giant by the name of Goliath came and harassed the Army of King Saul for days. Goliath supposed a wager which he would face the champion of Israel in single combat. The loser and their people would become slaves the winning champion thus putting to the war. King Saul and the soldiers were shaken in fear and had no answer until one day David came with gifts for his brothers and heard the threats of the Philistine giant. Saul in an attempt to motivate a champion from within his ranks offers a great reward for anyone who could defeat the Giant, so David offers his services.

When Saul looked at David, he viewed him with pity. However, David explained to him that he had the ability to defeat fierce beasts and had done during his experience tending sheep. Saul then offers David his armor. As he finished putting his armor on David, they both realized that David could not fit better yet even walk in his armor. It was at that moment David took off the armor and headed to the brook to get rocks for his sling. The story ends with David slaying the giant with a rock from his sling and becoming the champion of Israel (1 Samuel 17-51).

Notice in this passage David's demeanor. Though he was forgotten and overshadowed by his father and brothers, he mastered his place of solitude. It was in this solitude with his sheep that he discovered and built confidence in his gift. When his time came, he was certain that the Lord would empower him to defeat the giant. David could have tried to force King Saul's armor on his body and would have most likely been killed, but instead, he chose to engage in the fight of his life with assured confidence of his identity. On that day Israel did not need a knight in shining armor, they needed a Shepherd boy. Had David tried to play soldier, his would-be destiny would have surely ended with his death and the enslavement of his people. This is how important it is to protect our destinies as children of God. You do not need the mantle of another to fight the Goliaths in your life. You need the weapon which God assigned you from birth that has bought you this far, to this day and time in your life! It is that weapon which God will use to impact this culture in an incredible way.

Daniel's Confidence

One very important aspect of protecting your identity is refusing to defile it. Defile means to desecrate or spoil something. As believers, we have to find and then develop trust and confidence in who we are and who God made us to be. Developing this trust will ensure that we do not sabotage ourselves our purpose, or our mission. Notice Daniel purposed in his heart that he would not defile himself with the portion of the king's delicacies (Daniel 1:8). Daniel was given every and any opportunity imaginable to conform to the identity of the wise men within his culture. Remember his name, language, clothing, and food were changed. However, inside of his spirit, he purposed that the culture of which he was taken captivity by would not steal who God made him to be. Let me pause for a moment and ask you something. What have you allowed the world's culture to take from you? How much longer will you allow your identity to be stolen?

Identity Theft

Identity theft is one of the fastest rising crimes in America. Every year, hundreds of thousands of people become victims of attacks that aim to steal portions of their identities to rob them of their prosperity. The perpetrator's behind these crimes engage in various sorts of attacks to obtain your personal information such as phishing scams, spyware, and deceptive telephonic calls. The results of these attacks at times leave victims with a recovery process that in some cases can take months to years to figure out. To avoid such atrocities from occurring, companies now have trainings which they offer to employees and individuals to teach them how to properly guard and protect themselves from identity theft. The training may cost you time, money, and comfort but the end result is peace, security, and safety knowing that what belongs to you will stay with you; allowing you to live your life without fear.

Oz the Identity Thief

The culture of the day is itself a master of identity theft. Remember Oz needs your buy in to maintain his image of power. The power of Oz is only as real as your belief in it. That's why the image is the key. The image is bright, illustrious, and beautiful. Just as scammers take aspects of who you are, the Oz's of culture are masters at doing the same. So where might you find Oz? That's a good question. I have found that in life the toughest areas to navigate in life have been the grey areas in life. What are the grey areas? I can tell you for a fact as a young believer or a young adult they will be plentiful and will vary from person to person. However, for the sake of the book, my personal and professional definition of a gray area is simply a place of question, suspicion, and even fear. Gray areas are indefinite.

There are moments and seasons of life in which you have to truly believe and trust God, usually with very little to no evidence or direction. Due to the increased vulnerability to failure in these seasons of life, if you pay attention this is when you will be attacked the most. Consider Jesus. Before his ministry began in (Matthew 4:1) Jesus is led by the Holy Spirit into the wilderness for a period of 40 days. Having gone so long without food, the devil saw this moment as an opportune time to attack him. He first began to test Jesus through his flesh, by trying to tempt him into turning the stones into bread, Jesus rebuked him and fled. Satan took Jesus to the pinnacle of the temple of Jerusalem and through manipulation of scripture attempted to get him to jump from the temple in an attempt to end his life. Jesus refused to be tempted. Finally, Satan took him to an exceedingly high mountain and offered him all the kingdoms of the world, if Jesus would bow down and worship him. It was at that moment that Jesus rebuked him saying, "it is written thou shall worship the Lord thy God and him only shall you serve". It was after the final attempt that angels ministered to Jesus and refreshed him (Matthew 4:1-10).

Notice in this passage Satan attacked Jesus during a fast in the wilderness; a moment he believed that Jesus would be susceptible and weak in the flesh. He then tried to play on Jesus' pride (which did not exist) by questioning his sonship and urging him to practically commit suicide, which would end his mission and purpose on Earth. Lastly, he tried to offer Jesus the kingdoms of the world in exchange for worship. However, Jesus knew who he was. Jesus knew that he was the son of God. He had a secret ambition linked to a secret mission and divine purpose. Jesus knew that the kingdoms of the world and fullness thereof were already his. The savior of the world knew that there was nothing Satan could ever offer him to steal his identity as the Son of God!

Consider these truths. Then ask yourself what kept Jesus so deeply grounded? Notice as he was tempted, he consistently referred to what the word of God said each time. Furthermore, he understood his purpose, and identity were in the sonship of God. In his moment of vulnerability, he leaned on two things, the word of God and his relationship with God. Remember God's word is a lamp to your feet and a light to your path. If you continue to walk in the light you will have the illumination you need to navigate the grey areas in life. Never allow the enemy to exploit the moments of uncertainty in your life.

Resisting the Appeal of False Identity

At the age of 6 years old I was convinced that I would be an officer in the United States Army. I had watched every war movie classic you could ever imagine and would often run around the house emulating the actions of war movie actors such as John Wayne and Clint Eastwood. When I turned 18 and left to join the military, I struggled to adapt to the reality of what I believed a soldier was and did, to what was actually occurring around me. I spent a lot of time alone because of it. One day in advanced training, a soldier who shared my living quarters with me instructed me that I needed to get out of the room. At that time, I just stayed in while everyone went out to the clubs, bars, etc... He told me if you want to meet people and have friends you can't be a square. I lightly listened and thanked him for the talk but chose to remain in the barracks and watch tv. However, that night he came into the barracks with alcohol and told me to come outside with him. I went downstairs and to my surprise, there were several young ladies and some other soldiers from my company sitting on the back stairs of the barracks drinking.

I was 19 at the time and was just sitting there chilling. In my mind, I felt good. It felt good to be accepted. Shortly after my roommate instructed me, I had to drink. I denied his request. The group soon became involved. After about 5 minutes of pressing, I took the cup and drank. My roommate congratulated me and said see, this is what soldiers do. We work hard and we play hard. 10 minutes in I went from goofy and laughing to dizzy and falling. The night ended in my roommate carrying me upstairs. When I woke up, I felt guilty. I knew that my parents and most importantly God would not be happy with me. However, in my mind, I also felt good. No longer was I alone every day in solitude. I was happy to be accepted. But was I accepted for me? Or for being something I wasn't?

As I transitioned into Military College, I carried the habit with me. I took on the idea that soldiers worked hard and at night partied and drank. My mind was altered to believe that this was the culture of the Army. This is what soldiers did, so that is what I did. The habit would follow me afterward and would soon become a stronghold of addiction which affected my professional habits. On multiple occasions, I would show up to work hungover, reeking of alcohol. A fellow officer approached me and told me he could smell it. I told him I could handle it and that I was still excellent at my job. He said that's the problem. You're a functioning alcoholic, the worst type of alcoholic. I ignored him but his words hit me. How did I go from a good kid seeking to honorably serve his country, to a party animal consistently showing up to school and work smelling like a half-pint? I had lost sight of who I was. Somehow the identity and vision of that six-year-old serving his country with honor seemed so far away.

How did it happen? how did it go this far? I had ruined my credit spent all my money on alcohol and my grades were terrible. I had officially hit rock bottom. However, in late 2011 I went to a New Year's church service and the evangelist/prophet Steve Sampson spoke to me and saw that God saw me. He stated God sees you and your heart. God is about to visit you. You will read his word and understand it like never before; and will hear his voice like never before. Literally from that day on my desires changed. I felt a feeling I hadn't felt for years. My grades shot up, my physical fitness level increased, and the Lord instructed me to move to Texas.

Today, I am an honorably discharged military officer with commendations. Futhermore, I am a minister, and an educator with a high level of academic and professional education. For years I had lived under a false identity. However, it was the Rhema word of the man of God in my lowest point of life which started the transformation process leading me back to who I was really called to be. A man of honor, integrity, and purpose. Maybe you started well. But like me, somewhere along the journey, you lost sight of who you truly were because culture told you that you had to be something you weren't to be what you wanted to be. Don't look at the hating who you are. Humble yourself, and the Lord will exalt and restore you. He will place the ring on your finger, and sandals on your feet. Jesus will put a coat around you and kill the fatted calf because you were once lost, but when broken and humble before God you are found!

The Power of Sonship

If a doctor were to line me up side by side with my dad, they may or may not believe he was my father. Although there may be similarities in our appearance, the truth would remain inconclusive. In fact, I have seen watched documentaries about people who were adopted as kids seeking their birth parents. When they finally meet the person or people, they believe to be their birth parents the first thing they do is assess the visual appearance, looking for outward similarities. Though this is all good and well, nothing can be confirmed until a DNA sample is taken from the parent and child and studied under the microscope. It is the matching of DNA which confirms the relational standing of the child and their parent. As humans created by God, we have inside of us what I would call the "God Gene". This gene is a genetic marker that identifies us as sons and daughters of God. However, not everyone is aware of this gene's existence. To know and understand our relational compatibility with God we must first receive Christ and his Holy Spirit. When the Holy Spirit dwells within us, he confirms with our spirit that we are the children of God (Romans 8:16). This same Spirit teaches us and guides us in all things, and even endows us with the power to do God's will for our lives.

Notice that the ability for a mere human to walk with power on this earth is all linked to their understanding of who their father is. Jesus himself said he is the vine and we remain in him and he in us we would bear much from; but apart from him, we can do nothing (John 5:15). When we understand our identity, we live from the position of sonship. We become a powerful and formidable threat to the kingdom of darkness because we understand our father has given us power and authority to be movers and shakers in this world. I wish I could tell you that there was a plain and simple answer for discovering these powers but there isn't. For Daniel, they were discovered during his time of slavery, when he separated himself and sanctified himself from the Babylonian culture. He learned his purpose and of his gifts in solitude but demonstrated them publicly. Maybe you don't feel like a Daniel in today's culture, maybe you don't feel gifted. If that is the case, I tell you as Paul told Timothy; stir up the gifts inside of you (2 Timothy 1:6). This does not mean the gift is not already inside of you, at times we just need to be reminded and reaffirmed through the laying on of hands or by exhortation. Remember to stay connected to the vine and understand apart from God you can do nothing. However, with God, you have access to all things pertaining to life and Godliness. Never forget this power is inside of you and operates through your spiritual DNA. It is a representation of the "God Gene" inside of you. This is the power that will allow you to discern, navigate, and influence the culture of which we live in.

Conclusion

Your identity is one of the most precious gifts from God. You must protect it at all costs. Throughout life, you will find that many threats will arise in attempts to alter, distort, and even steal your identity from you. As a believer it is vital that you remain aligned and connected with the vine, that is Jesus Christ. As your relationship with Jesus grows and your faith in who he made you to be blossoms, you will then operate at the highest level of gifting. That operation is from the level of sonship. Sonship (including daughters) is the proof and verification of your DNA. That is where your culture-changing power comes from. It is all where wisdom, discernment, understanding, and the ability to do signs and wonders come from. It is already on the inside of you! Now God is stirring an awakening inside your spirit so that you will learn to operate in these gifts like never before. In the last days' fleshly attempts to create and influence change will no longer work, the flesh does not have the power alone to create the change needed in this new age. No, it is the decisive power, fervent, and effect Rhema word will be what breaks the yokes and chains of the Oz's in this world. Finally, remember, God has given you everything you will ever need to be everything he has called you to be. You do not need the right clothes, the right swag, or to manipulate and rub shoulders with the right people to make an impact. Your identity is linked to your gifts, which are found through sanctification and seclusion before God. Once the gift is activated inside of you, it is that gifting that will take you places you never dreamed of. You will even stand before the great people of this time. Don't trust your own intuition, stir up and trust the "God Gene" or the gifting of the Holy Spirit inside of you. Remember, it is not by might, nor by power but by the spirit of God inside of you. Walk in your God-given identity, be you, be great, and you will change the culture of which you live for the kingdom of God.

Keys to Remember:

- Your identity is linked to your destiny.

- If you betray your identity, you betray or deter your destiny.

- The "God Gene" inside of you is the power to operate in your gifting.

- Your gifting operates through the understanding of sonship not through the flesh.

- Protect your identity at all costs, and you will walk in your destiny.

Epilogue

If we as believers are to be effective in these days to come, there is much preparation that must take place. This type of preparation will require sanctification, fasting, prayer, and a listening ear to the voice of the Holy Spirit. As I prepared to write this book, I considered my own relationship with God and the rhythm of my own spiritual life. I found that most often the Lord reveals the deepest mysteries and dreams to me usually around 2-4 in the morning. I have learned to write them down and cherish these sacred moments with God. These downloads vary from person to person but if we take the time to get alone with God and listen, I believe we are all capable of receiving them. You can hear the voice of God! It is that voice that will allow you to discern the Oz's behind the curtains of your life. Furthermore, that voice will allow you to receive his instructions concerning his will for your life.

Remember, everything you need to change the world around you is already on the inside of you. You don't have to try to be something you are not or assume the identity of another individual. Safeguard your identity. Walk in the ways of the Lord and he will be the lamp to your path. You are called to be light. Light is used in many ways; most of which involve the finding of what's unseen. If we walk in the light as Christ walked in the light, then those who live in the spiritual darkness will be able to find the light of the world. It is him (Jesus) they should see in us.

As it pertains to influencing culture, remember we are not only called to be light alone, but salt as well. However, you don't just take a whole bunch of salt and dump it all over your food, do you? No, you add, then taste, and continue until you get the flavor you want. This is what Daniel modeled during his captivity in Babylon. Each time he was called before the king he added his measure and the wicked magnified God. Daniel was effective because his heart was right. He knew his identity and did not need status, promotion, riches or praise to be validated. He found his identity in who God made him to be.

Finally, it is my prayer that these words have impacted you as much as they have impacted me. The Lord has shown me that he is raising up a generation of young believers who will have the ability to see behind the curtain of the wicked agenda of Satan in today's world. These people will shake regions through their ability to see, discern, and provide understanding to the lost, dying, and hopeless. They will not walk in pride and insecurity, but like Daniel, Shadrach, Meshach, and Abed-Nego will stand in unison, gracefully defying the Oz's of this word and the false images they are using to ensnare the souls of millions. Though you are young many will seek you for answers. They will see your love, they will see your mercy, they will see your grace, and they will see your heart.

In closing, I pray that the Lord grant to you wisdom and skill in all learning and literature; and the ability to understand images and dreams. May you live with integrity and model the light of Jesus Christ. Never chase an image, never let an Oz lead you into the world of imagination. Have faith in God made you to be and you will influence culture like you never imagined. Thank you for reading this book may God bless you and keep you safe until the return of Christ, amen.

IF YOU ENJOYED THIS BOOK, PLEASE TAKE A BRIEF MOMENT AND LEAVE A REVIEW.

Notes

1. Baum, Frank L. *The Wizard of OZ*. Ed. Baum. Chicago: George M. Hill Company, 1900. Print.

2. https://www.eliyah.com/lexicon.html

3. https://www.biblegateway.com/

About the Author

Justin Littlejohn is a secondary educator, with a strong background in leadership, serving 7 years as a military officer, and over 10 years in young adult and college ministry. He holds a M.A in Management: Organizational Leadership and is the founder of the One Way Initiative. He resides in North Houston, Texas with his wife Jamie and their four kids.

CONNECT WITH JUSTIN LITTLEJOHN ON:

Website: www.onewayinitiative.org
Facebook: @authorjustinlittlejohn
Mail: P.O Box 2307 New Caney, TX 77357